Gail Fitzpatrick

W9-BPK-311

"I loved this book. Sheryl Lain pulls you pell-mell into the heart of teaching, where her writings (jottings and poems to her students and for herself) sustain her through parent censors, faculty fist fights, shattering personal moments. The result is a memorable illumination of her students and the teaching life."
— *Miles Myers, former executive director of the National Council of Teachers of English*

A Poem for Every Student

Creating Community in a
Public School Classroom

BY SHERYL LAIN

National Writing Project
1998

National Writing Project Corporation
Copyright 1998
All Rights Reserved
Printed in the United States of America
No part of this book may be used or reproduced in any manner
whatsoever without written permission, except in the case of brief
quotations used in critical articles or reviews.

Please direct reprinting requests and book orders to:

National Writing Project
5511 Tolman Hall
University of California
Berkeley, CA 94729-1670

Telephone: 510-642-0963
Fax: 510-642-4545

Library of Congress Cataloging-in-Publication data available.

ISBN: 1-883920-11-6

Design & Layout: Paul Molinelli
Cover Design: Roxanne Barber
Cover Photos: Elizabeth Crews
Editor: Art Peterson

Sheryl Lain, director of the Wyoming Writing Project and a teacher in Wyoming high schools and junior high schools since 1968, comes from a family of teachers going back to her great grandfather and grandmother who taught in one-room schoolhouses at far-flung locations around the Rocky Mountain West.

She is married to a teacher, Gayle, and two of her four children are also teachers.

She is a published poet and creative nonfiction writer and has coauthored with Gayle an illustrated Wyoming history, *Wyoming, the Proud Land*.

for my students

All students' names and some circumstances in this book have been altered to protect the identities of those portrayed.

Contents

CHAPTER ONE

Writing Lessons

DECIDED to be an English teacher in tenth grade, sitting in Miss Petty's English class.

It was spring in Wyoming, late March, when the weather is anybody's guess. One day we might have a blizzard — snow blowing white, horizontal lines outside the window. The next day Miss Petty might open the window, inviting inside the green smells of budding trees and grass. *Zephyr* was a vocabulary word I learned that year. When I said it, I thought of little puffs of air blown from the cheeks of God. Spring in Wyoming meant blizzards and zephyrs.

After a long Wyoming winter, spring snapped me awake. Everything was more potent, even the words on the pages of our *Adventures in American Literature* anthology. When Robert Frost's "Two roads diverged in a yellow wood" lodged in my heart, I decided, then and there, to be an English teacher. That way I could live forever in the beautiful world of words. Maybe I could help students feel the power of language.

That was in 1960.

When I started my practice-teaching with ninth graders in 1966, I soon realized the huge difference in classroom points of view. Standing at the podium looking *into* student faces was not at all like sitting in the student's desk, Row One, Seat Five. Secondary school is a crucible heating up over a Bunsen burner. As the temperature rises, the organisms wiggle and squirm, becoming more and more agitated. Those kids wrestled the spotlight away from Robert Frost.

I hit on the idea of writing about my students and about myself, their teacher, as one way of examining our school predicaments and staying sane.

Pimply-faced Robert was one student I noticed. During my eight-week student teaching stint, Robert wet his pants. One day, after the *brrriing* of the bell and the bolting-for-the-door ritual, the girl next to Robert called my attention to a yellow puddle in the contoured seat of his wooden desk. That puddle became a symbol. I came to understand that my students were much more than young minds awaiting my breathless words of enlightenment.

Those kids, with all their needs and wants, their quirks and foibles, took center stage.

When student-teaching started, I was in the late stages of weaning our baby. I soon realized I was like Robert, bringing to class my own needs and wants and quirks and foibles. This little poem addressed my predicament.

Student Teaching
My milk came in every time the bell rang.
Pavlov's dogs had nothing on me.

At home, my mom jostled my baby during our weaning,
while I learned to balance on the high wire
juggling classroom and family.
The regularity of my body's rhythms was the only
*   certainty.*
No college training for this:
Live kids wiggling and creating waves of chaos
and Robert, a ninth grader, who peed his pants.
I was next to useless
so boggled by all our bodies' distractions.

3

Writing about the quixotic teaching life probably saved my sanity…and my teaching career.

My first teaching contract in 1968 was in a tiny high school with 13 students in the sophomore class, each of whom was different from the other twelve. When I handed out the grammar book, the students looked as if I were challenging them to a dual. But while Donna and David in the front row wore a sort of grim grin on their faces — like they knew they'd win the fight, however distasteful — Richard, Chuck and Wanda in the back acted whipped. That day, I began to learn about "individual differences."

To make sense of what I noticed, I wrote about how the kids reacted to my lessons.

I noticed that my Native American students wouldn't raise their hands to answer questions. Not simple yes-no questions, not thought-provoking questions. They acted like raising their hands to vie for teacher attention, wrestling it away from some classmate, was unseemly behavior.

I also noticed that spelling tests advantaged the student who could already spell, the ones who barely glanced at the words and got 100s anyway. I noticed that Richard and Chuck, who couldn't spell and couldn't conquer grammar, wrote crystal clear metaphors that took my breath away, while Donna's and David's attempts sounded dull as irrigation-ditch water.

All this noticing affected my teaching. I still gave those spelling tests, we still worked through some of those grammar drills, we still followed the story of American literature from the Puritans to the present. But I began to have students write more and do fewer drill worksheets. I gave individualized spelling tests. I brought in *Black Elk Speaks* and *A Raisin in the Sun*, a break from the steady diet of the anthology. The change was probably imperceptible to my principal who observed me twice that first year. But I *felt* different.

Besides tinkering with the curriculum and my delivery of it, I started to make little jottings about my students. I wrote to make sense of my experience. The writing helped me sort out my ideas. Somehow the writing changed — maybe *charged* is a better word — my relationships. I wrote about Weldon, for instance, and I was *with him* in a way I hadn't been before, as he shuffled in my room, grinning bucktoothed, walking down the aisle.

My poems to each student had their genesis during my first year of teaching as I sought to make sense of the whirlwind.

When I first walked into that classroom and stood up in front of all those eyes, I felt under attack, sensory attack. So many messages on so many levels. I had an articulated job description, to teach students American Lit or Brit Lit, to teach them various types of writing, to offer them speech activities. I knew my content, and I was ready for *that* job. But the unarticulated job, the one no one talked about, was the most difficult and important: to know my students so I could teach them. I needed to know the curriculum, the textbooks, my calendar, and my lesson plans. But all of this was so much baggage without human relationships. If I had no content to teach, my students and I might as well stay home, but if I had no awareness of those I teach, content lost its power. Now, thirty years down the yellow road, I see more clearly how the noticing and the writing about the students affected me as a teacher and the Weldons and Roberts as students. Gradually but persistently, I filled up one yellow legal pad after another.

At first, I didn't share these musings with the students. But I did write to them, the way language arts teachers do, giving them personalized word gifts as I responded to their writing. I scrawled stars and smiley faces up and down the margins of their poems and stories, their essays and research papers to show them where their words leaped off the pages, bursting like Fourth of July fireworks in my heart.

After a while, I wanted to give students an even more potent writing gift. So, I started a gift-giving tradition. At the end of the year, I gave each student a little brown paper bag and a pile of note-sized papers. We used these supplies to write notes to one another, composing quickly to get one done for each class member during the period. "There are two rules," I said. "Be nice and be specific. Name something that you notice or admire or remember about each person. We'll mail them into the brown bags before the bell rings. Get ready, get set ... go!"

Throughout the years, only one boy absolutely couldn't, or wouldn't, write to his classmates. Calvin was aloof, unconsciously convinced of his superiority. While I scribbled, I watched him struggle, start, stop, struggle, start, stop. When kids began mailing their notes to him, he was still frozen. It was then he realized that, though he couldn't think of nice things to say about his classmates, they sure could think of nice things to say about him. When that realization hit him, Calvin started to cry.

The next day he brought a note for each of his classmates.

Once, Lloyd, a teacher in my building, asked me how I knew the messages were kind. "Do you read them first?" he asked. Up to that point I'd never read a single message addressed to anyone but me. His question planted a seed of doubt, so I glanced at some of the brown-bag messages left on the window ledge for kids who were absent. From the first slip of paper to the last, the notes followed the guidelines: They were nice and they were specific.

Years later, students tell me they still treasure their brown bags.

In those days, I wrote notes for my students, but I didn't, as I do now, give each of them a poem.

Twenty years into teaching, I participated in the Wyoming Writing Project. My classmates and I met six hours a day for two weeks. The teacher did not lecture. And she was, she explained to us, not the "teacher" but the "facilitator." Instead of listening to teacher talk, we practiced. Every day we wrote for an hour, after which we shared our writing in small groups. At the end of the two weeks, we published one piece which we read aloud to the whole class. Then the facilitator gathered our writing together and made a class anthology.

After the Project, it seemed necessary to go public with my writing. After all, I expected my kids to publish, so I should, too. The idea lodged itself in my head, waiting for the right moment.

The next year, I was teaching eleventh and twelfth graders in a college-bound composition class. The students' writing was going nowhere. It was Thanksgiving and I was depressed. The most recent papers — expository essays — were terrible.

Their pieces seemed less alive three months after school started than they did the first day. My nonstop teaching of structure and rules had pretty well clogged up their voices. So I decided to teach poetry awhile, hoping that this exposure would limber up students' nonfiction writing.

Our focus on poetry led to a spur-of-the-moment lesson. I asked kids to pick someone in the room and turn her or him into a metaphor. "Add lines to extend the metaphor," I said. My suggestions to the students as they were composing grew out of a piece I was jotting at the moment about Jude, a boy in the third seat of the first row. This boy perplexed me because I saw so much potential in him, yet he gave so little. Looking at his dark, handsome face sporting a clean line of mustache, I visualized him as a sheik, robes swirling around his legs as he strode through his sheep and women. Looking at him and writing, I saw him, right in the middle of a hot, sandy desert. The timer went off, signaling the end of a three-minute quickwrite. There was Jude, back in his little brown desk in our little brown room, not at all exotic nor romantic.

The kids shared their pieces about one another, those who wanted to, and then they insisted I share. I asked Jude's permission and he gave it with an indifferent shrug of his shoulders.

As soon as I started reading about him, he was no longer diffident. He became intensely interested, stretching, peering through the surface reflection of the words to see what I really meant. It was almost as if he were trying on a jacket in front of a three-sided mirror at a department store. He was looking front, side, back, to see how the poem fit, perhaps imagining himself wearing the poem around in his head. Evidently he was comfortable, because his face relaxed, his lips turned up. He asked me for a copy.

Jude, the Desert Sheik
Today at school
an unformed lump of clay
stuck in the mud of his own definition.
But inside
a red-cloaked gypsy
striding Zorro steps,
an Arab stalking
through swirls of sheep and women
scarlet passion firing jet-black eyes.
Alas, a desk again
so trivial a domain
to contain
his rich red blood.

After I read the Jude piece, the class was dead silent. Dana broke the silence. "I wish you'd write one for me!" she said. Kevin chimed in. He wanted one, too. "I'm afraid of what you'd say about me," joked Dylard, a royal pain in the posterior most of the time. He tried to mask his real desire that I'd write him one, too.

Of course. How could they resist reading about their favorite subject — themselves. So, during odd moments, while the students worked their way to the end of the semester, I jotted poems for each of them.

That was almost ten years ago. Now I write a poem to every student, publishing right into their hands. Giving my students poems has led me to pay more attention to them, adjusting the tone and length and topic to fit the students without stepping too close into intimacy. In the process I discovered a surprising side benefit: lines of trust spun like a web across my classroom. One visible sign of their closeness as a class was Kyle. Everyday he came in and promptly turned his seat sideways so he could see both me and the rest of the class. Gradually the students made a messy sort of circle of their chairs. Always dramatic, Sophia crossed the threshold into the classroom and threw her arms wide, as if to embrace us all. "You're all invited to my house for a real Mexican Christmas party!"

As I've noticed and written to them, I've become even more aware of how each student is different and how they change like the mercury in my thermometer on the back fence. Also, as I notice and write, I begin to read my students, and I begin to make meaning out of the messages of their lives. The better I understand them, the better I can tailor my teaching to fit them.

We build relationships with one another, even though we bring to school different values, learning styles, and family backgrounds. We forge a community in spite of a school system that often treats us like assembly-line gizmos and our learning as unconnected and stripped of personal meaning. Some of us, the "stars" and "heroes," soar. Others nose-dive, if only momentarily. Together, in this place called school, we build relationships through our own writing and by reading the writing of others.

CHAPTER TWO

Relationships

WHEN I was a little girl growing up on a homestead in northern Wyoming, I wrote. I had a diary which could only be opened by my younger sisters on pain of death. But writing in that diary was insignificant compared to writing letters to my grandma, 500 miles away. As soon as I learned cursive, Dad appointed me the official family correspondent. He said, "Make her feel like she's right here with us on the homestead." When the envelopes from Grandma started appearing in the mailbox out by the bridge, he scrounged up an old straw fisherman's basket to hold her letters. That fisherman's basket was my first writing portfolio.

In my letters to Grandma, I worked on the craft of writing, shaping the phrases, sounding lines in my head, moving my lips as I read. I wanted her to see Heart Mountain with the sun setting behind it, smell the wind in the bed sheets fresh off the line, and understand my life, balanced between farm and school. Writing to her made me realize how much I loved the shape of my days. Morning and evening on the farm bracketed school, comfortable, interesting school.

These letters were like a mirror. In their reflection, I could read my life. Somehow, the writing shaped me. I didn't write to her about the time I broke the overhead light fixture with a broom handle, chasing one sister or another through the house, or the time I mortified our shy hired boy, teasing him about girls. Somehow, the process of screening what to say to Grandma helped me perceive the difference between honorable behaviors and obnoxious ones. Grandma and I wrote back and forth until the day she died.

As my relationship with Grandma grew through the letter writing, I became subconsciously aware that writing connects people. Now as an adult, I consciously use writing to bring a classroom together and, hence, to become more productive.

After almost thirty years teaching school, I remember all kinds of students — those who connected with one another in spite of their differences, those who strained the boundaries of our relationship, and those who acted as bonding agents. My grandma and the students continue living inside my head.

Doug Forgot He Wasn't Home

In the ninth grade, Doug called me "Mom." He was so immersed in his work, he didn't even realize what his mouth had said. I've thought about that peculiar teacher feeling, sort of like a parent's love, but not really the same. We probably need to coin a new word for that teacher warmth partially hidden behind the red grade book.

12

I wrote about Doug and these feelings in my teacher journal:

"Mom,"
he called me.
At his age, too,
no baby, newborn into first-grade rows
and chalk-dusty teacher talk.
I love you, Doug,
you fresh-mouthed lunatic,
tangled in teenage fears and longings.
Love your tender-skinned babyhood,
your callouses on the way to now,
your place ahead where I see you.
I smile inside,
answer in teacher voice, puffing white chalk dust,
camouflaging the tenderness
you'd mistake for weakness.

13

SOPHIE WITH OPEN ARMS

Once they get used to writing regularly, students' lives shout off the page. Each student, diverse as a thumb print, affects the classroom.

Sitting in the same class across from each other, Eva and Sophie were antonyms. Eva was a cool, lanky blond; Sophie, round, brown and effusive. Sophie had lots of extended family. Eva had only her parents; they hailed from Kansas City and from somewhere else before that, always chasing the American dream, leaving extended family far behind. Eva took honors classes in her north side junior high — an elitist through and through. Sophie, on the other hand, survived school only to the extent that she could wrap her arms around some teacher or idea.

Of the two, Sophie was easier for me to like, but harder to teach, for she had to love the topic to write about it, she had to love the book to read it, she had to care about the discussion question to stay focused. Eva, on the other hand, knew she could shine if she did the prescribed work. She calculated just how much effort to expend to get the A in this board game called school.

I wrote this poem for Sophie, wanting her to know that I noticed her acceptance of all of us.

Sophie
speaks Spanish at home.
Sofia she is called by her parents and grandparents.
Her black hair
thick, alive,
Polynesian paradise.
If I inhale
when she swings by,
hint of coconut, papaya, kiwi. She is brown and round
    all over
chocolate fudge
sweet.
She and her girlfriends come from the south side
and sit together facing cool blondes whose shirts and
    socks match.
All Sophie's friends are brown, too, and warm
wiggly
prone to sitting on desktops

talking out
combing each other's hair
touching.
Eva and her friends
are self-contained
hold legs and lips together
pencils poised over open notebooks.
By Christmas vacation,
Sophie
enters
throws wide her arms,
"Hey you are all my friends now!
This is my favorite class
and you are all invited to my New Year's party."
I breathed a sigh of relief.
In spite of all your differences,
you showed me that our
class finally jelled.

NATHAN SHARED

I believe in a classroom that listens to each other's voices, but I hold my breath, a little, when I ask, "Who'll read?" wondering, What if no one volunteers? What if the subject is a little touchy for the school room?

One day when I asked, "Who'll read?" Nathan's hand shot in the air first. As he walked down the aisle to the reader's chair, good-humored kids high-fived him. "Way to go, Nathan!"

From the beginning of his reading, Nathan's voice and face took us high up the mountain switchbacks — two cousins in his dad's pickup, Nathan driving without permission, rear tires spitting gravel into the dusty air. The corners were sharp, the traction bad, but the boys, being boys, were impervious to danger. Nathan's story captured the freedom of that moment.

But the next second the pickup lurched airborne off the lip of the road. The boys' smiles froze, then spilled out round OOOO's of fear as the truck flipped and landed on the brink of the world, wheels spinning in the air. Nathan read, "We crawled out of the broken back window, safe and sound, but Dad's pickup was totaled."

Suddenly, Nathan's face crumpled like twisted metal. He put his hands over his face and his wide 15-year-old shoulders shuddered. He was crying right in front of us!

We held our breath. My own vision smeared, like I was looking at him through water.

"Do you want to go to the rest room?" I asked him. He kept his face buried, as he lunged for the door, the manuscript forgotten on the floor. The class was silent.

Kellie stepped quietly up to the author's chair. She bent and picked up Nathan's manuscript. Then she sat down and paused a moment before she started reading her own piece about her grandpa's farm. Kellie was perceptive like that, knowing how to ease the awkwardness. She was into the second page when Nathan stepped back over the threshold. I saw him pause when he saw Kellie reading, relief on his face. He slid into his desk and began listening to her story about Kansas cornfields and farm breakfasts with pancakes from heaven. When she noticed Nathan, she skidded to a stop. "Will you finish yours now, Nate? Or I'll read it for you. I don't mind stopping, really."

Nathan finished reading, this time from his own desk. He told how the boys were so lucky, how guilty he felt risking his cousin's life that way, driving without permission from his dad. A lark gone awry, that's what it was.

After the last line, the class murmured, feeling for him, understanding his guilt, knowing, somehow, that Nathan's wrongdoing was absolved a little because he wrote about it.

Jon spoke, breaking the quiet at the end of the reading. "What I wanna say is how you wrote that so strong. You were, like, moved by your own words. Seems like you were just as swept up as us. Like, you were reading what happened to someone else. Then the feeling hit you unawares."

The class murmured agreement.

"Well, I was, you know, touched by how honest you are." Christy's blue eyes were sincere. "I mean, how you told it, not holding back."

"Yeah, you trusted us." That was Robin's voice.

"Well, you're alive, Nathan. I'm glad." Alisha had the softest voice and people softened to hear her.

Kellie, still perched in the reader's chair, gauged the class and Nathan's face. "You guys. Let's do a cinnamon roll hug on Nathan?" She'd taught us how to do this big group hug a few weeks earlier when someone in the class had moved away, something she'd picked up in her improvisational theater troupe.

Most kids laughed, some moaned, but they cleared their desks away to form a circle of bare floor space. Nudging Nathan into the middle, they held hands, forming a long line. Nathan turned around and around in the middle and the line twisted, becoming a circle enveloping Nathan in the middle. "Now, squish forward, everyone," Kellie said.

"Too touchy-feely for me." Royce stood outside the big circle, arms folded across his chest to contain himself. I figured he'd unthaw later in the year, maybe. Already he smiled, toler-

17

ant as a father, as the rest of us goofballs group hugged, celebrating Nathan's sharing and his survival.

Doug Bites the Hand that Feeds Him

Eva and her clique were aloof and challenging to get to know, but they were a piece of cake compared to Doug.

Some people wake up on the wrong side of the bed all year long. Maybe they feel better after they've blown off a little steam. Or maybe they constantly need to dare life a little so they can feel more alive. Students with this kind of attitude create a tension in the classroom, make it hard to get the work done, much less get along with one another. Doug was a person with splintery edges, a boy whose idea of a relationship was a wrestling match.

Every day, Doug begged to be disciplined. One day I blew up.

Doug,
like my neighbor's Doberman,
you kissed my hand in the hall today,
the same hand you bit last week
before I lashed out,
grabbed your shirt
buttons popping all the way down the hall.
I hauled your 6'2" frame
to the principal.
After the explosion
the classroom was silent as a cave.
This week all week you've been cherubic
till today, Friday.

I notice your knife edges sharpening again.
Vaccination didn't take.

As a freshman, Doug had the build of a man. Weighing in at 185 pounds, he was an Apollo of a kid with a good-looking face and rich, dark hair. But, oh, how miserable he was. His mom abandoned him — too much responsibility, maybe. She wanted to be a ski bunny in Jackson. After she left them, Doug and his dad retreated off the mountain to lick their wounds. They moved to Cheyenne, living with Grandma.

I don't know how Grandma stood Doug, he was so rude. Once, I saw her out my window after school. She waited 45 minutes out there in the drop-off lane while he goofed around in the halls somewhere. I imagined him yelling and trying lockers to find an unlocked one. When he finally got kicked out of the building, he went up to the car and yelled at her for parking too far away from the door, making him walk a few extra steps. He slammed the car door so hard the window in my classroom seemed to shiver.

I lost it one day when Doug was battling me for control of the class, throwing rocks into the quiet pond I was trying to create. I had been gone from school due to an extended illness. While I was out, Doug ruled seventh hour. The sub was glad I came back.

After the absence, I knew I'd have to reconnect with the students, and I knew it would be hard. They'd be surly, thinking I'd abandoned them. So I pulled out a journal-writing exercise from my bag of tricks. Doug played along for five minutes. Then he cut loose a sound suspiciously reminiscent of a fart. Phhhh! He dropped a tiny rock in the quiet classroom pool. A tiny ripple. I looked his way. The students went back

19

to their journals. Within a minute he belched. Uhhh! A bigger rock, a bigger ripple. This time I went over to stand near him. That's when he shoved the dictionary off his desk. Bang! Sounded like gunfire when it hit the floor. Deep in their writing, the students jumped out of their skin in suspense. The ripple was a wave.

I saw red. Grabbing Doug out of his seat, I heaved him out the door and down the hall to the office, forcibly dragging the big lunk. In the principal's office, I aimed his body toward a chair and gave him a shove. Later, I remembered to breathe. My legs buckled as I headed back to my dead-silent class.

After that episode and for several weeks, Doug carried on like I was his hero. He even kissed my hand in the hall once. Reminded me of the neighbor's Doberman, how the only way a human can have a respectful relationship with that animal is to prove he is the head canine. When Doug's dad came in for a conference, I got the feeling that his son bewildered him, though he hid his vulnerability behind a huge, ex-football player facade. Maybe he was glad someone at school put her foot down, acknowledging that his angry son was almost out of control.

I hated how I reacted so vehemently, but Doug, a football player just like his dad, understood blocking, tackling, and superior field position. He did relinquish his power over the room — albeit temporarily.

Within ten days he was back at it, tapping on the walls, windows, door of our relationship, wanting another show of emotion, the only kind of affection he recognized. At the end of the year, he wrote a sort of mixed-up piece reflecting his mixed-up feelings about his relationship with me and his classmates.

Dear Mrs. Lain,
I remember trying to pass English and I still flunked.
Trying to make new friends and always ending up with

the old ones. I remember getting in a fight over a girl.
When I was sent to Mariah Junior High, everyone thought
I was cool. Getting caught smoking right out in the lunch
yard. My English teacher, Mrs. Lain, not even giving me
a chance in English and I did try hard. Mrs. Pru, my
eighth-grade teacher gave me a fair chance and passed me
even though I failed. She liked me. I wish all teachers
were like that. (What I said wasn't true. Mrs. Lain gave
me more than a chance.)
Doug

21

The Dougs of the world make it hard for a class to bond so that together we can get to the heart of teaching and learning. On the other hand, folks like Nathan and Kellie make relationships possible.

I've never been able to tell precisely at what moment a class jells, but one day I'll look up and realize that the circle of kids has turned toward one, and the work of the class continues without my incessant orchestration. The magic happens, partly because of the sharing — reading aloud, writing reflections, and teaching one another.

ADAM, THE ADHESIVE MAN

The class gets to the Jell-O stage partly because of students like Adam, the glue holding a group together. I wrote to him about this uncanny ability to adhere us.

I'd pay to have a boy like you in class.
What would every day be like without you there in the
      middle
forging links

between Christie in the front row and Joe in the back?
You said you don't read
much,
but
when we read Fahrenheit 451
you said Montag's love of burning
is just like everyday hallway vandalism.
You are the glue that holds life together
in this room.
I'd like to bottle and market you for
every
classroom
office
home
meeting
workplace
I'd get rich.
Do you know and like everyone?

It was Adam's idea on the gift-sharing day before winter break to have everyone read out loud the poems I'd written for them. He asked his classmates if they would. They assented. Afterward, after the silence, Adam asked, "Mrs. Lain, how'd you nail each one of us like that? I didn't know you knew us so good."

To which I thought: How could I help it, Adam? I've read your work all semester.

Adam's reflection of the course, written right after the final exam, speaks to the power of building relationships in the classroom. He wrote:

Dear Mrs. Lain,
There are many different types of people in this class.

Since there were so many it made it fun when we were doing class discussions and projects. It's a lot like the world and all the different people in it. Our English family has different races of people just like the family of mankind does. Everyone has a different view just like all the people in the world have different views.

One memorial thing that happened in our class was when we had John run the Gauntlet. When John ran through, some kids hit him while others let him through. I think the Gauntlet represents life in a way. When you are running through some people will try to knock you down while others will try to help you.

Another memorial time was when Stephanie told the class about that man who was stalking her. The whole class felt mad that nothing could be done to stop him. The class wanted to write letters to the legislature to try and get a law passed against stalking.

Another moment was on Chris's last day of school. Everyone gave him a big group hug and told him good-by. In our class there is a lot of love and compassion.

If there was more love in the real world like in here I think there would be a lot less crime and violence.
Adam

Adam's letter was a testimony that our classroom had become a congenial community — a vital step if we were to learn together.

TREVOR'S QUIET POWER

I felt the power of Trevor's personality, subdued as it was. All the kids felt it, too, in the air around him as he sat and walked and thought and talked. Trevor had charisma, and he was completely unaware of it; he was unconscious of his own impact on people, unconscious that he became the center in everyone's eye. I knew him in and out of school, for my son coached him in American Legion baseball. I'm certain he did not know he carried so much authority, that he set the tone for the class or the baseball game just by his carriage or his casual remarks. He was self-effacing when I read this poem to him.

24

Trevor
you are the eye of the storm
the vacuum in the whirlpool's vortex
the center which others circle.
Eyes directly or indirectly
glance at you for the way to go.
You are calm
seeking no attention.
Still you are the center.
To accept the banner others expect you to carry,
this is your life,
like it or not.
Wherever you go,
on baseball green diamonds,
or in dark underground tunnels a miner's helmet the
only light,
or in bright white operating rooms,
your presence will always be felt
and eyes will glance
your way.

Trevor read my poem and decided to write back to me. His response was humble, just like him.

Mrs. Lain,

You remember me as the eye of the storm? I don't think so, I don't even want to be. But I'll think about it. Sometimes I get the feeling you know what we do before we do it.
Trevor.

BETH ANN, THE BALM OF GILEAD

Certain students, like Beth Ann, help settle a class. If I don't have a Beth Ann in class, I try to help cultivate someone to play the role. Every day, unobtrusively, Beth Ann slipped into the room, into her seat, and the class quieted. Her presence was a calm hand stroking an antsy horse. As I wrote this poem to her, I squinted my eyes to hold her image right in the middle of my forehead so I could catch the essence of this remarkable girl.

25

Beth Ann,
a Southern belle's name.
Sweet as sugarcoated drawl
soft as shade-dappled skin.
She's definitely not Wyoming
bouncing over rocks
catapulting into spring.
She moves sedately in a green world
dropping white magnolia kisses on quiet ponds.

She loved the poem, she said, because, as she knew I knew, she was reading *Gone with the Wind*. Beth Ann smiled in her new-found awareness that she was a serene, calming influence on all of us.

ELLA GRACE IN DIRE STRAITS

I knew Ella Grace as a freshman. That was ten years ago.

I saw her the other day. The apartment house she lives in was up for sale. A friend, a potential buyer, wanted me to go with her to have a look. The three rooms were decorated floor to ceiling with sagging boxes. Ashtrays overflowed staleness. A little blond two-year-old met us at the door. In her teeth the baby clutched, mother-kitten style, her bottle filled with some thick pink stuff reminiscent of Pepto Bismol. The husband or live-in boyfriend, draped in the only chair, must have been at least ten years older than Ella, toothless already and as unkempt as the apartment. Ella herself snatched a quick look at me and then tucked her chin to her chest, pretending to be washing dishes, hiding her face and those blue eyes from my view. I didn't cross the distance between us.

My friend decided not to buy. But the picture of what had become of Ella was hard to erase from my mind.

I remember Ella in junior high. The lounge talk had the scoop on the Boggs kids. Mom on welfare, not much more than a baby factory, they said. Already Ella's big sister, about 16, had a kid. All of them lived together.

In ninth grade, Ella's black fake leather jacket smelled of old tobacco smoke. Her nails were never clean, but she dazzled me with a happy grin and lasered me with blue eyes alive with warmth. Poetry was her favorite kind of writing, and she had a natural sense of rhythm and word play. The research paper loomed large on the horizon. No way would Ella keep track of all those note cards, all those deadlines. Organizing all that stuff linear-like was beyond her. But the weight of the paper in the teacher's grade book was heavy — if she didn't do it she'd flunk.

I assigned her a permanent place in the room where, before school, during home room announcements, and at lunch, she could work on her thesis — that panda bears had a right to survive. Her research paraphernalia never left the premises until almost the deadline, giving her less time to lose the cards, the rough drafts, the articles. Some days we both stayed after school, each of us working along on our own projects. I got the feeling my presence helped her stay on track. I assigned her a classroom support group. Everyone was vested in everyone else, because of The Bribe. I'd buy pizzas if *all* the papers came in on time.

As the deadline drew near, Ella would have to take at least the rough draft home and recopy it. Would she do it?

She did. She told me later she did it, not for the grade, but for the class to get pizza. "Who cares about the grade?" she asked, her eyes sincere.

I wrote her this poem:

Ella Grace
I teach you
and you add a grace note to the day
I ask you to do what is alien to you
be methodical
be organized
"I don't write neat," you say.
Indeed, you don't think neat.
But you think and write rainbows and unicorns
I insist on the research paper.
You have no intention of writing it
at first.
"If all the papers come in on time, I'll buy pizza."
It's a blatant bribe I offer to help you and those like you

27

to pass.
You do it.
For love you do it,
but not to be organized methodical promoted.
Ella Grace, a grace note in my day, I agree.
For love I too would trade all the gods of organized and
methodical.

I didn't know much about the personal details of Ella's life really, beyond the lounge gossip. So when I got a letter from her later that summer after her ninth-grade year, I wasn't sure exactly what she meant when she said, "Thanks for being there when I needed you." Maybe there was more to her story; there usually is … much more. I remember a course I took from a social worker one summer at the university. She quoted some data I now wish I had. Something about how the vast majority of at-risk kids — more than 80 percent — claim that, during their hard times, a teacher was their source of inspiration, their model. The interesting thing is, when these kids were asked if the teacher knew about their personal problems, 70 percent or so said, no, the teacher did not know. Now, most teachers do know more than the kids think. But many troubled kids see their teachers as anchors in the storm, and these teachers need not know all the nitty gritty details of their lives to offer strength and hope. Just our presence is enough, if we show acceptance, understanding.

Anyway, running into Ella Grace living in such dire straits felt like seeing a former student's name in the police blotter in the local newspaper. A wave of helpless frustration swept over me. I'd hoped this girl would not end up lost in some morass without an anchor. But she isn't done living yet. Remembering her generosity of spirit and her willingness to work for the good

28

of the group gives me hope that, to paraphrase Faulkner, Ella will not merely endure, but prevail.

DEAN DIED TOO SOON

Dean Rusk was on his way into school. He drove his own car, because early mornings he helped his dad on the dairy farm. He figured he could work longer if he drove his own vehicle in, save the hour and a half bus ride. His car sped along the quiet two-lane every morning, up and down hills following the undulating golden ribbon of road paint. This one particular morning Dean, blinded for a second by the rising sun, hit a tractor crawling along the highway. He died instantly. I never got to show him the A on his poetry, the comments on the freshness of his language, his metaphors. "You are the first teacher who liked my writing," he'd said only the week before. He always thought he was dumb in English because he couldn't spell.

He was my first student to die, and I cried like he was my son. That was my first year of teaching. Over the years, I've attended other students' funerals, and I still feel that thick, tight pain, like a coiled rope around my larynx.

Dean Dies
At the funeral
the preacher mentioned Jesus, the fisherman.
You skipped school a few times to fish.
Now I'm glad:
You had so little time to cast.
In your memory,
I watch a fish break surface.
I note the poignant arch,

the momentary glistening in the sun
before the iridescent flash slips back into mystery.

It broke my heart, and the hearts of my students, when Dean died too young. Still, something in us yearns to bond, one human being with another, no matter the pain of potential loss.

Writing bonds people. Disconnected people like Doug who didn't anchor himself in someone else's life, who remained unattached — didn't learn as well. And if he did learn, he had no way to make it matter to anyone. On the other hand, Sophie, Adam, Trevor, Beth Ann, and Ella — those kids settled into the work of the classroom with satisfied sighs.

I learned how writing can forge relationships clear back when I corresponded with Grandma. The letter writing made me a writer, someone who reaches out to someone else with the most powerful tool the human mind ever devised — language. Likewise, the poems to my students, and their writings back and forth to me and to one another, helped the students bond, and they became much more proficient writers, too. Writing does double duty that way — it causes us to grow closer, while at the same time it makes us writers.

As time moves us through the semester and my students' writing and reading improve, I watch their learning unfold before me. Nathan and Kellie sit out there, concentrating. Their faces screw up, thinking of just the right word, trying out the sounds in their heads. When they reread their sentences, eyes moving across the lines, lips unconsciously forming words, their faces sort of melt. It's a sight to behold, reminding me why I choose to stay in school, years and years after I graduated.

30

CHAPTER THREE

Values

As the classroom becomes a community, the group is somehow greater than the sum of its parts. But the parts are still important. A teacher holds a double vision — building a community and focusing simultaneously on the individuals who make it up.

Noticing students means reading their values that shout off the pages of their writing. Their beliefs are written all over their papers and their bodies — in their haircuts, their clothes, their issues. Jennifer shaved her head. Zach shaved a Z on his skull. Deidre sported tight, midriff-length T-shirts, and Dan wore cowboy boots.

As a child I, too, wore my values like a suit of armor. One of my issues was fairness. I've had a thing about fairness ever since I was little.

Janet Jacks sat next to me at the banquet for our thirtieth class reunion. She looked worn out. I'd heard she was battling cancer.

Between bites of mashed potatoes and roast beef, I asked her if she remembered the time in fifth grade when the skunk got loose in their house. She remembered. Said the skunk smell was so potent, even the baking powder in the cupboard carried the taste into future cakes, long after the house was aired.

I remembered that after the skunk visit, Janet and her brother and sisters stayed home from school three days, bathing in tomato juice and hanging their clothes outside on the line. When she returned to class, she still carried a hint of the skunk visit. I liked the way she smelled. It reminded me of summer.

However, Miss Bostrick, our fifth grade teacher, didn't like skunk smells.

Now, Miss Bostrick was gray. Gray hair, gray dresses, gray eyebrows, gray chin whiskers. Today, I wonder about her life, even feel a little sorry for her. Maybe she had too little of girlhood, no giggle fits, no glittery snow angels. But in fifth grade, I thought she was gray. Her teaching was gray, too. Our gray pencil lead filled in a thousand miles of lines on endless worksheets.

That day, when Janet stepped to the classroom door, quiet as a mouse, the room was ready for her. All the desks were squashed over into one corner — under the American flag. All except Janet's. Hers was acres away, by the open door. All alone.

If Miss Bostrick was the epitome of gray, Janet was head-ducking shy, pale pink shyness to the nth degree. I never heard her volunteer an answer in school, and we were together from kindergarten to graduation. Her soft blue eyes were shy, her freckle-dusted skin was shy, even her light brown hair was shy.

Clear over there was Janet, so visible. Like standing on a stage with no lines to say and no props to hide behind. I began to seethe. By morning recess I'd reached the boiling point. Colleen, Kay and I burst into the rest room, me on a rampage. The opposite of Janet, I was a spittin', yellin', stompin' kid. "Can you believe it? Janet stuck clear over there? Imagine how she feels, a sore thumb like that? I hate Miss Bostrick. She's a mean, old, sour puss!"

Just then a toilet flushed. A metal latch released its hold on the door. Miss Bostrick's square frame filled the whole doorway. I ducked my head expecting a blow. None came. I sneaked a glimpse of her face; it was expressionless, like she never heard my tirade!

I sat on the edge of my seat the rest of the day, waiting for retribution, but Miss B. paid me no mind. The next morning, though, the chairs were back in ordinary rows. From my place between Carol Briggs and Jimmy Baird, all alphabetical, orderly, I looked over at Janet. There she was, back between Amy Jacks and Kathy Johnson. Just like nothing happened.

What Miss Bostrick thought about me I'll never know, but I'm sure she noticed my armor glaring in the sun, just as I notice my students' values.

JAKE HATES UNFAIRNESS

Jake was more like me than I was. Of all the students I've ever had, Jake was the most vocal in his violent allergic reaction to anything unfair. Since injustice happens at school all the time, Jake was often upset.

He was hurt when other kids were insensitive or downright cruel. He was mad at teachers who, in the name of keeping order or getting kids to pass, used bribery or threats. Jake rolled his eyes when teachers would threaten, "You are going to flunk my class if you don't turn in the research paper." He refused to play along when teachers (myself included) bribed: "If every single one of you turns in your portfolios, I buy pizza."

Jake was true to his motto: "The ends do not justify the means."

What Jake believed is with me still. No matter what pressures are pressing in on me — if I need to get the curriculum covered come hell or high water or if I need to keep the kids from climbing the walls or if I need to keep my flunk list short so I don't hear from the principal — I think how Jake'd disapprove if I cut corners.

He's right. These control tricks aren't very satisfying for very long. See the kid over in the corner dozing, the one with his head resting on his arm, his wrist dangling off the edge of the desk? That one tells me that teacher tricks were tried before in first, second, third grade, long before he hit high school. They failed to spark an interest in learning then; they sure don't matter now.

Jake wanted school to be more than a checklist of things to do to get the high school diploma, and all the bribes and manipulations, all the victimizing and categorizing rubbed him wrong. He was incensed that school sanctioned unfairness. After he read the poem I gave him, he told me that having someone understand him meant a lot.

> *Jake*
> *The first day of first grade Jake sat at lunch next to a*
>   *girl who talked*
> *against the rules.*
> *He turned to answer and got caught,*
> *red-handed,*

his mouth in the middle of forming a word.
Teacher made him stand,
hand covering his mouth,
all lunch period.
She forgot him there.
His white bread dried out
along with the hope his mom had that morning,
smiling, "Have a good day!" at the door.
Jake
hated the kids in second grade who circled Jamie
on the playground
making her play pig in the pigpen,
a game designed to have her crawl around in the mud.
Jake knew Jamie's story. His mom told him,
how Jamie had a stroke before she was born,
leaving her left side saggy, always trailing her right.
Jake
threw up every day in fourth grade reading class.
Mrs. Addley became conditioned, nudging the garbage
pail his direction at 9:45 every morning.
The teacher was impatient with slow, old Mark
Trudeau, who already knew he was dumb.
When Jake's mom called Mrs. Addley about the
habitual upchucking,
the teacher said she had no idea why.
Jake
cringed inside when the long-term sub in fifth grade
dumped Angela's desk out
on the floor,
crayolas, homework, gum, scissors,
in a sad heap.

She said, "You won't have a mess at school
like the one you live in at home."
Jake's face fell.
Is it any wonder you contemplate
dropping out of school?

Knowing students like Jake, who live their beliefs, caused me to remember Janet Jacks and her skunk episode. At our thirty-year reunion, I asked her about it. She said that, oh, yes, she remembered all right. Then looking me square in the eyes she said, "Sheryl, you always did like things to be fair." Guess I'm not the only one who notices people's values.

GARY SAVES FACE

Jake shared my idea of fairness, but Gary's values weren't exactly consistent with mine. A handsome senior, Gary sat in my first English class back in 1968. He was part Shoshone and part Mexican American. The desk was pretty tight-fitting, physically and psychologically, for Gary. He looked like a man, and he thought of himself as one, showing off to the other seniors by flirting with me a little at the Homecoming Dance. A few weeks later, near the end of October, Gary came to class sick, or at least that's what I thought. His head lolled from side to side. Suddenly, he threw up all over the desk and down on the floor. Without a word he stumbled out of class. He refused to return to school.

Later, I learned that he wasn't sick, exactly; he'd gotten drunk on the one-hour-long bus ride from the ranch.

"Why won't he come back?" I banged on the counter in the office and screwed up my face at the principal. "Make him and his folks come in for a meeting. Gary needs a high school diploma!" I didn't understand why the principal and the more experienced teachers wouldn't fight for him. The Gregorios came in for a meeting, but I had the feeling that all of them were humoring me. They acted like they knew something I didn't know, something as obvious as the nose on my face.

Finally, someone patiently explained to me, the outsider, that Gary *couldn't* come back. Not once he'd lost face. Getting drunk wasn't so bad, but not holding his liquor and barfing in my room, that was bad. I tried to make sense of Gary's behavior by writing about him.

Gary
liked to prove his machismo.
So
he couldn't tolerate his stomach's weakness.
Coating his desk in vomit meant he'd quit school.
Quit —
seven months before the end of the race.
Gary, the punishment doesn't fit the crime.

It's tricky to really care for students with values so alien to my own. But learning their reasons helped me to accept them.

RICO THE ANARCHIST

Years after I knew Gary, I met another Native American boy, Rico, a Sioux, who brought his values to school, too. All students do, but Rico wore his in neon. Landing in my class his ninth-grade year, he sat as far away from the rest of us as he could. He parked himself next to the blackboard, laid his head down on the desk, and turned his face to the wall. That's what he did every day for the first two weeks. Out in the hall, I stopped the guidance counselor and asked her about changing his schedule. "I'm not getting anywhere with this kid. Would he work more for a different teacher?"

No, she assured me. He'd almost certainly flunk no matter what. His whole school career was pretty dismal, ever since his parents' divorce in sixth grade.

I thought about this boy, how his behavior, though quiet, screamed, "F___ you, world!"

"Well, if he is going to be in my English class, then he needs to be in my journalism class, too. Maybe a double dose will help him. Or at least jog him out of his catatonic trance."

She looked at me like I'd lost my mind, but agreed to change his schedule. She told me a little about him, how his dad divorced his mom and married someone else. Rico flip-flopped back and forth between the two parents, and in the process got lost.

In the third week, after he'd dropped study hall and joined journalism, Rico begrudged us with a tiny communiqué on the chalkboard. Using little pieces of broken chalk, he wrote "Anarchy" in sharp, angry letters. I took note of his first halting steps to communicate with us and started writing little notes to him on his papers. After that, Rico's mental checkouts became rarer until he joined us most of the time, putting his head down only during spelling tests. "I'm such a bad speller," he complained, "I confuse the spell check!" Finally, Rico hatched. In journalism, Rico teamed up with Daniel and Erin, two other independent thinkers, and published a bizarre little underground newspaper with editorials telling the truth about the world and calling for radical reform of everything, from schools to the presidency.

I wrote to him.

Rico,
your haircut alone
turns off half the clean-shaven world.
On each paper, especially spelling tests,
you write ANARCHY in deeply imprinted letters.
No school seat contains you
for long.
If the rows are too straight
you put your head down and leave.
Your favorite theme is freedom.
You consider dropping out of school,
your idea of the ultimate freedom.
I wish I could show you
how to hold a balance
between order and chaos.

Rico wrote back. Indeed, his spelling would confuse a spellcheck, but his message was sincere.

Mrs. Lain.

    I'm greatfull for all you have taught me. I realy needed
that lecture that time in Dr Jensens office. You are a very
important person in my life. You are totaly write abought
'to beat a system yu have to learn all you can abought it.'
That is totaly write.
Rico the Anarchist

Rico graduated from high school. The last time I saw him he was spiffy, all starched up in a white shirt, working in one of the business offices of the Holiday Inn.

DANIEL THE PASSIVIST

Daniel's whole family waited to fall apart until he was in ninth grade. The breakup meant he had to move from a private parochial school with twelve students in his class to our school with 1,300 students. The divorce and the move were a double whammy for this bright, sensitive boy. I was lucky enough to have Daniel in both my journalism and my English classes, in the same classes with Rico.

Later, when he was a senior in high school, he came back to ask a favor: Could he live with me and my family until he graduated? By now Daniel's long hair hung midway down his back, and his blue jean jacket, a walking billboard, sported more print material than our local newspaper. His jeans were old and meticulously slit and frayed, revealing hairy, snow-white legs.

My brand new student teacher, sitting at my side planning the semester, gulped. Is this what teaching is about, taking in strays?

Dan really was homeless. His mom had no place to live any more, so she camped out with Verna, Daniel's sister.

My family, whittled down now to my husband and our youngest son, Jade, voted to let him move in. I think Jade was lonesome for his siblings who had gone off to college. But by the time my family gave me the thumbs-up, Daniel had already found couch space at a friend's place.

I remember Daniel in ninth grade. How he wrote convoluted and complex prose. How he spoke passionately about preserving the purity of the American Constitution and the Ten Commandments. In his world suddenly cut adrift, these two documents felt to him like strong anchors to hold him secure.

One midwinter day, I held up before the eyes of the class an essay contest sponsored by the National Rifle Association. My students had to publish, meaning that, at the very least, they had to read some writing out loud. I encouraged them to enter writing contests, and every time an announcement came to my attention, I went fishing in my classes, looking for takers.

This particular writing contest had Daniel's name written all over it: Defend the Second Amendment to the Constitution — a citizen's right to keep and bear arms. Plus, a $1,500 savings bond went to the first-place winner.

Daniel won first in the nation. The gist of his piece was his passionate defense of his lodestar, the U.S. Constitution, a pure point of reference for him, and, in his opinion, for all Americans, in this chaotic, diverse society. We need, he claimed, a few solid ground rules around here so we don't go zinging off the globe — no gravity to hold us earthbound at all. His motto was: "That government which governs best governs least," and he reminded his readers that Hitler gathered up the guns.

By spring Daniel had allowed his hair, and his tenacious hold on certain literal translations of his holy grails, to grow out.

> Daniel
> won $1,500
> in the National Rifle Association contest
> defending the Second Amendment.
> This spring
> the national photographer came to give you the savings
>   bond
> and take your picture for the magazine
> By then you'd grown out your hair to chin length
> and outgrown your literal interpretations.
> "I'm a passivist," you told me.
> "Don't believe in guns at all,

just in freedom from government control."
In the picture
the national winner is a boy with long, straggly hair
blue jeans jacket, a walking billboard,
"Anarchy" written in black magic marker,
frayed jeans that look like a Rottweiler played tug of
   war with Levi and won.

I'm sure many readers of the NRA magazine thought Daniel needed a barber, but the prize money wasn't wasted on him. Last time I heard about him, he was in graduate school, working on an M.F.A. in writing.

BEAUTIFUL DEIDRE

Another one with values alien to mine was Deidre. Deidre adopted her values right out of *Cosmo*. She attended school just enough to keep abreast of the gossip. Beyond that, she had no use for it. She never paid any attention to me. Once in a while I called on her to answer a question. I always had to repeat the question, and she always gave an interesting, albeit inappropriate, response. Her attention was as slippery to grab as a newly-landed fish.

When Deidre did come to school and enter the room, all the students, male and female alike, watched her, unconsciously holding their breath a second. She swayed to her usually empty desk in the south side of the room and commenced to comb her hair, or Sophie's. Deidre was a capable writer and often told about her sister who was in prison for manslaughter. Her jail sentence was wrong, wrong, wrong, claimed Deidre. That guy's death was an accident. The sister was merely driving away from the bar and her so-called boyfriend. He shouldn't have been hanging onto the door handle of the pickup truck when she stomped on the gas.

From the time Deidre was in elementary school, her sister groomed her for beauty pageants, figuring with such good looks, Deidre could come out on the top of the heap in this jungle called life. Then they could move out of the trailer park and onto Park Avenue.

Deidre sported a perfect zero in my grade book, which was OK by her. That was pretty much the case in all her classes. She told me not to worry: in her life she would not need school. I gave Deidre this poem.

> *Deidre*
> *tries out for the Junior Miss Pageant.*
> *When she comes to class*
> *she parades down the row like it's the runway,*
> *her chest uptilted for the boy judges.*
> *The girls and I, we're backstage crew.*
> *She is breathtaking—*
> *periwinkle eyes, sunyellow hair*
> *pulled straight back in an uncurled ponytail,*
> *whipping cream skin,*
> *her face swept clean of paint.*
> *She considers English irrelevant*
> *compared to the spotlight.*
> *"Pageant winners usually have to sport a decent GPA,"*
> *I advise her.*
> *She waves away my words*
> *like so many gnats.*

My words of warning to Deidre had as much effect as a drop of water on stone.

CARLENE THE APOSTLE

Most high school kids are vehemently opposed to censorship, but Carlene, the daughter of a preacher, *wanted* me to censor. Her classmate, Chloe, studied Christ symbols for her research project. Afterward, Chloe was forever connecting her findings with other literature, even *Fahrenheit 451*'s character Clarisse, a "sacrificial lamb" if Chloe ever heard of one. However, any mention of Christ at school rubbed Carlene the wrong way, and she dropped me a note at the end of class one day.

> *Mrs. Lain,*
>
> *I know you say you are religious. But in here you give kids with different religions a chance to talk. And you don't seem to mind. Chloe talks about Clarisse like she was Christ? Give me a break! You tell creation stories from other religions. Do you think Genesis 1 is just another story? Well, it isn't. It's the gospel truth. I would just like to know one thing, Mrs. Lain: Do you believe that Jesus Christ is the one and only Lord and Savior of all mankind? Because nothing else will do.*
> *Carlene*

Most teachers face unhappy parents who question certain reading selections or students like Carlene, ill at ease with values not literally their own. No matter, I have to share literature and have students write — and these activities cause people to think, maybe, heaven forbid, unorthodox thoughts. At the same time, I have to nurture relationships among all of us in the classroom. A delicate balance.

I wrote this little zinger for Carlene and gave it to her the next day after she dropped off her note addressed to me.

Carlene
our class is full of kids
proud they've outgrown Sunday school:
Dylard, his tack-sharp wit punctures everyone's bright
*   blue idealism;*
Mannie experiments with temporary shortcuts to
*   heaven.*
Working on Big Ideas,
we do get around to God.
I know Christ as a symbol
is out of the question for you.
Funny
you of all people would rather leave all schooltalk of
*   Christ*
alone.

Carlene didn't buy my line of thinking. At semester, she left our class and transferred into Business English, where presumably her values weren't tested.

JASON THE QUIET KNIGHT

When Carlene threw a fit and checked out of our class, Jason didn't say a word, but his eyes looked straight at me, almost speaking out loud. "Blow it off, Mrs. Lain." Yes, Carlene's rejection stung, but Jason's silent, clear message helped reassert order and reason.

Jason drove into school from his ranch 45 miles out on Horse Creek, and he was never tardy. This kid did not have a lazy bone in his body. When the big research paper loomed on the horizon, he decided on his thesis — a defense of using Wyoming rangeland for cattle raising, in spite of an Eastern environmentalist's idea to return the prairies to their natural state.

> *Jason,*
> *a smile tugs my heart*
> *seeing you in my mind's eye.*
> *You are gallantry,*
> *a silver-armored knight in dusty cowboy boots*
> *attuned to horse and prairie.*
> *Clear eyed*
> *you accept the challenge*
> *to stand for right*
> *even today*
> *where dragons to slay*
> *threaten all existence.*

46

School boards, city councils, state houses—all these would benefit from guys like Jason who support sensible, balanced perspectives.

DAN, HORSEBACK PHILOSOPHER

Dan was a cowboy, too, and Jason's best friend. A nicer pair of boys would be hard to find.

When we read poetry, Dan's body language spoke for him: he pulled his lanky legs tight under him and shifted his eye contact to the top of his desk. He was suspicious of poetry; it didn't make sense to him. One day we finally read a poem his heart understood, and then his mind caught on. It was Wendell Berry's piece, "The Peace of Wild Things." Dan said it seemed like the poet spoke inside his head. Like Berry, Dan, too, felt overwhelmed by the human world and soothed in nature. He ended up writing some poetry of his own, and it sounded like a blend of Berry and Dan.

Why?

When I watch the news on TV
The only headlines I hear are sad
Two children kill a baby
Woman is raped
Plane crashed, 100 killed
When I hear these things my heart sinks
But then I think of the mountains
Evergreen trees sawing in the wind
Wild animals peaceful and free
Fast flowing rivers racing and splashing
A warm feeling spreads through my body
Why can't the whole world be like this?
And how could it ever change?

47

Dan worked summers on his grandpa's ranch fifty miles from nowhere. While his horse rested nearby, he'd string silver wire from fence post to fence post, completely at ease with his solitude. Once, Dan and I shared stories about people we'd known who would come visit us from cities. He told about this guy, Bruce from Detroit, who came out to the ranch. Dan said he seemed jittery, especially when they went out to the pasture to round up a couple of horses. The whole time Bruce kept scanning first the horizon, then the sky, like he was expecting a bomber to fly out of the blue and strafe him. Answering Dan's whistle and the promise of oats rattling in a rusty Folger's can, the horses spilled over the crest of a hill, galloping in. They scared Bruce out of his wits. Dan said it seemed like Bruce mustered all his courage to stand his ground as the horses barreled straight for them. Dan figured the guy was weird to be so nervous.

I told Dan about a friend of my husband's from Pittsburgh. They'd met in grad school, and Gayle invited him out to Wyoming. They went to Gayle's favorite fishing stream forty miles south of Laramie. Instead of noticing the beauty, the way the rocks balanced one on top of the other, like a natural cathedral, the guy commented, "Why would anybody live clear out here? I feel sorry for them."

Dan felt the same way about city folks. "They just don't know any better." That's what he thought every time he took cows to the Denver Stock Show, truck and trailer battling traffic on I-25. "Why would anybody live here? I feel sorry for them."

"I guess it's all in a person's point of view," I said. We both shook our heads.

He didn't say anything when he got his customized poem from me. But Dan wasn't one to say much at all. He scanned the lines, and then he looked up at me with clear hazel eyes, wise and calm as his horse's.

> *Dan rides.*
> *The Wyoming prairie is his business.*
> *Sagebrush brushes the underbelly of his horse,*
> *scenting the dusty air.*
> *Its memory lodges —*
> *a permanent definition of home.*

Our beliefs show in the writing and speaking. They speak up in what we wear, how we settle into tasks, whether we slouch or sit up straight in our desks. Jake, Gary and I railed against injustices we bumped into at school. These clean-spirited values diverge from school practices. Daniel understood the paradox of his ideals: no gun control, not because he liked guns, but because he believed people should honor the Constitution and govern themselves with intrinsic controls. Deidre and Carlene, though their beliefs took them in opposite directions, still refused to listen to anyone else's reason, so stuck they were on the values they brought from home. Jason and Dan did listen to reason, and their minds seemed to grow without growing pains. For all of us, our values are right there with us as we work together in the classroom.

Chapter Four

Apron Strings

I ALREADY missed my two little boys — and that was two weeks before school started!

Mr. Dunham and Mr. Sackman knocked on my front door one late August afternoon. Dressed in dark blue suits and matching white shirts, they looked like vacuum cleaner salesmen. And they acted that way too — courteous, expectant, smiling. When I opened the door, I glanced out at the curb and saw a light blue sedan with "School" on the license plate. Turned out, the superintendent and principal were looking for a last-minute English teacher to teach in their tiny district forty miles away from home.

My boys, Darol and Tagg, were three and six years old. I didn't want to leave them at day care all day, worried about what they'd miss — loud giggles, races through the house, and on-the-spot cuddles.

But my husband and I had college expenses. My National Defense Student Loan was due and payable. I chewed my bottom lip. Yes. Yes, I'd be the solitary ninth, tenth, eleventh, and twelfth grade English teacher of about 75 students. But I negotiated for a schedule more suitable for my family. I'd work mornings — teaching four classes in a row. Bang, bang, bang, bang. Then I'd come home to be with my boys.

From the first planning days, I missed the family. But over time I learned that when school works, it, too, is a source of family. This became the story of my life as a teacher. After 28 years, I still try to connect with students the minute I pick up my class roster. My eyes dart down the list. Oh, there's Richard Tobler's name — maybe he's Maddy's brother. Hmmm. Todd Hammond. I wonder if that's the boy whose mom works in the school cafeteria.

For me, this process of creating family begins the first day and lasts all year. It's part of the curriculum. Besides teaching, I want to know, really *know,* every student.

No one actually sat me down and taught me this. I just missed my family while out there at Wind River High School in my first teaching assignment. My own children were in morning day care, my husband was teaching at the local community college, and I was in a place among strangers. So I set about making school more like home, getting to know the kids … and their parents.

ROD: FROM BLACK HOLE TO BIG BANG

Invisible to the naked eye, Rod's family sat right there next to him at his desk. For Rod, just the word *family* conjured up a deep well of feeling — the pain tangled together with the love.

Rod's sister had leukemia, and he'd suffered so much during her long illness. After she died, her pain ended, but his didn't. Everything he thought about, directly or indirectly, was related to purging his sorrow or making sense of her death. During the research paper unit, Rod picked the origin of the universe as his topic. Though I tried to persuade him to narrow the scope of his study, he just couldn't. I figured that somehow Rod's choice of a topic was connected to his sister's death, and he needed a very broad lens in order to try to understand. Writing for Rod was healing.

I watched Rod's thinking unfold during the six-week research project. Toward the end of school, I gave him this little poem:

> *Your older sister died of cancer last year.*
> *You grew up through those months*
> *of her long agony.*
> *Now you want to know about the beginning of the*
>   *universe.*
> *You study Big Bang Red Shift Black Hole.*
> *You're a ninth grade quantum physicist trying to figure*
>   *things out:*
> *Your mom's faith has Sister Jeana in heaven somewhere*
>   *with God.*
> *You want to know for sure.*

He wrote back to me:

> *I remember the first time I walked into your room*
> *this year. You didn't know this Mrs. Lain but I was a mess*
> *— messed around with drugs the summer before. I guess I*

was scarred about Jeana. My folks didn't pay much atten-tion to anything but Jeana before she died and afterward they were lost in a fog. Well, I feel better now. Got a handle on things. Football, my job, school. This class was hard, but I'm glad I did my Big Idea on the beginning of the universe. Funny how my science piece kinda had a God feel to it. I let myself think about Jeana now.

I tried to show Rod, by word or deed, that I didn't pretend to know all the answers to his big questions. But I honored his struggle to untangle all the strings and find some answers. Teetering on the edge between chaos and order, he responded. Slinging his load over his shoulder, he pushed forward on his journey.

THE ROOM IS BUGGED

Though Rod's family was an invisible influence in the classroom, the parents of my first students in central Wyoming were right there in my face.

Every day I left my babies and husband and drove west on U.S. Highway 26. During the forty-five minute drive, I thought about all the dynamics brought to bear in my new, expanded family. So many people's interests to understand and balance. How could one little school be so complicated? Would a bigger school be even more mind-numbing? I learned later, when I moved to larger and larger schools, that the smaller the school, the more parents I knew on a first-name basis. And the more intimate the parents' involvement, the better the kids performed.

But thirty years ago, I was groping along in new territory as a first-year teacher.

I wondered about school as I drove, so deep in thought that sometimes I ignored the view outside my car window. There

I was, smack dab in the middle of some of the most beautiful country in the world. The snowcapped Wind River Mountains paralleled the road on my left. One of the peaks was Gannett, reaching 13,804 feet into the sky, the highest point in Wyoming. Behind me the sun rose over the Gas Hills and Copper Mountain. Every time I glanced in my rearview mirror, I saw a different colored land. Purple shadows, orange air, gold-tipped winter wheat, silver snow.

Almost everything that happened caused me to pause, to wonder, including my first book-censorship experience. Some parents took exception to *The Grapes of Wrath* as appropriate reading material for their seniors. I was called before the school board. The farmers sitting around the table avoided my eyes. Their two-toned faces told their story. They rode tractors in their fields all day, their John Deere caps protecting their bleached-white foreheads, while their noses and chins were sun-red. Sunburn wasn't the only reason they looked flushed; they were blushing, embarrassed to talk about their concern over Steinbeck's novel. But it came out. No preacher ought to be having sex with his parishioners. And if a preacher did dive into the bushes with willing penitents, no writer ought to write about it. The superintendent told them that Steinbeck won the Pulitzer Prize, for heaven's sake. He wasn't an insignificant fly speck of a writer. Didn't matter. The board asked me to use another book next year.

Years later, I learned how to read the subtext of those parents' message. Nancy, a former student, told me the rest of the story. She was in my class when the parents took exception to Steinbeck, and she's still in that building, now teaching in my old room. We chanced to meet at a state language arts conference. I asked her about the flurry over *Wrath*. The real problem, she explained, was that the twelfth graders, suffering from acute senioritis, didn't want to work, and reading such a fat book was work. So they formed a conspiracy. Plant the open book in strategic places around their houses. Then hope their dads would read the passages, proclaim it trash, and throw a fit. They'd be rescued from work.

Ah-hah! The light went on. "So what do *you* have those kids read?" I asked Nancy.

"*Grapes of Wrath.*" She grinned from ear to ear.

"How do you get away with it?"

Nancy grew up out there. She knew all those good people from church, community pot lucks, and Eastern Stars meetings. And they had known her since she was in diapers. "I give the kids a choice of books. They can read *Grapes* or *Great Expectations* by Charles Dickens." She explained that she selected Dickens because he, like Steinbeck, wrote about rugged social conditions. According to Nancy, given the choice, the kids always picked *Grapes,* probably because it was more contemporary and authored by an American. Once they did the choosing, they kept their mouths and their books shut around the house.

Nancy always was a smart girl.

Years later, another parent's involvement felt like a slap in the face. Mrs. Clamden came to school to yank her daughter, Caitlin, out of my room. Caitlin claimed I had a penchant for nude males, said I drew a naked man on the blackboard. I, who can't even draw? I don't think so. Nevertheless, that was the claim. According to Mrs. Clamden, Caitlin kept a list of my "indiscretions" — took notes in class — and then shared them with her mom. Hence, said Mrs. Clamden, the claims were irrefutable. When the guidance counselor called me into a meeting with Caitlin and Mrs. Clamden, I brought ten years' experience into the confrontation. I read the unspoken issues more swiftly than I once would have. I knew that Mrs. Clamden, an ex-English teacher, had recently been released from her position in the district due to lack of class control. I was pretty sure Caitlin was trying, in some convoluted way, to help her mother. Maybe she was saying, in effect: "Here, Mom. Look what batty Mrs. Lain did today! You were never that bad." At the meeting, I assured the Clamdens, and the counselor, that I didn't draw nudes on the board. Mrs. Clamden kept her arms folded over her chest; Caitlin looked smug. The counselor and I agreed that Caitlin should transfer to another English class. A part of me honored Caitlin's loyalties, her ties to her mother, but her rejection stung.

The story didn't end there. About twelve years after Caitlin abandoned the ship of my classroom, her mother rang my doorbell at home. It was late on Sunday night. When I opened the door, the wind blew snow in my face. Not a good night to be out. Mrs. Clamden stood there, hair held in place with a cotton scarf knotted under her chin. She thrust a note into my hand. "I've wanted to ask you to forgive me many times. My minister said I should just go ahead and speak to you." After she left, and I collected my wits, I read the message she left:

Dear Mrs. Lain,

I should have called you years ago, but I didn't. Turns out Caitlin has a problem with lying. She's been a big disappointment to me. She's living with a guy in Denver right now, they're not even married. She doesn't live in reality, that's what I've figured. You didn't deserve the fit we threw in the office to get her out of your room. I hope you can find it in your heart to forgive me, but if you can't at least I tried.
Mrs. Clamden

Staying in teaching for the long haul, I've had a chance to learn to read between the lines when parents come calling, and what have I learned? That I don't need to take their issues as a personal jab in the ribs.

Darcy Keeps the Faith

Sometimes a parent's message, like Darcy Martin's mom's, reads, "Don't let my little chick hatch too soon into a world of fuzzy ideas, too slippery to get a grip on." Or another way: Mrs. Martin didn't want the cocoon of her family faith ripped open before her butterfly was ready to fly.

Darcy was a devout girl. The cherished daughter of carefully prescriptive parents, Darcy performed an admirable balancing act between her religion and the secularity of school. When Darcy was a sophomore, both parents came to school to check us out. Her father attended one full day, mostly to listen to the science teacher's view of evolution. Then, her mom called me to see if she could volunteer regularly in my classroom. I knew the Martins from community choir. Swallowing hard, I conjured up an image of Mrs. Martin, her hair tightly curled and her mouth painted pink and prim, in the midst of that group of sophomores: Chad from the reform school, Tom who couldn't sit still for ten minutes, Alexis who snorted every time I said the heinous word, "homework."

Mrs. Martin's was a loaded question. If I told her, "No, I don't need help in my room," she'd report to her Bible study group, most of them home-schoolers, this "failure" of public school. If I said, "Yes, come on," she might see more than she could bear. I decided she was welcome to come. "Start on Monday," I told her.

After the first day, she was disheveled in body and spirit. Her hair looked like a hat perched askew on her head. "Where'd you get all these ruffians?" she asked. "How did you get all the dregs of the earth assigned to you?" Though the Martins loved the Lord, they clearly did not love every one of God's creatures. I could tell she was afraid for Darcy in my wildly heterogeneous sophomore class.

"Just wait a few weeks," I assured her. "They'll come together, settle down. They'll care about one another and the learning." And they did. She saw it with her own eyes. Plus, after reading some of their papers, she discovered that nobody, not even "these ruffians," was so easy to categorize and dismiss.

I wrote Darcy about her ability to steer a middle course between the secular school life and her family's core beliefs.

You are the apple of your parents' eyes
They come to school to check out evolution
to see that creationism is given equal time
check out other evil influences rampaging through
*   public schools these days*
You are gracious
You understand how complicated everything is
You join hands holding one side and the other.
I admire you, Darcy,
calm-eyed, and accepting.
Long ago when my own answers weren't deep enough,
I remember meeting a student's or parent's clenched jaw
*   with my own.*
Now, I'd never dream of resisting you and what you
*   stand for*
let alone subverting.

Onward, Christian soldier,
in this slip slide slosh pit world.

I figured out Mrs. Martin's agenda, and Mrs. Clamden's. The bottom line was that they wanted me to honor, even love, their girls. This concern was at the heart of all their other issues, like grades, success. No problem. What she wanted was what I wanted— to love Darcy and Caitlin as part of my school family. This meant I, too, wanted to shelter them a while from rude awakenings. Remembering the angst I felt when my core values ran smack dab into wider world views, I'd rather ease my students into the water instead of throwing them, fully clothed, into the deep end.

STEINBECK THE SCAPEGOAT, AGAIN

Schools are in the spotlight today. And the more society suspiciously eyes schools, the more folks like Mrs. Martin ask permission to come inside and see for themselves what's going on. I invite them in, but I realize their presence can cause complications because their agenda and mine are different. In this case, the mother's agenda was to control her daughter, while mine was to ask her to test some ideas. But we do have something in common: we both love the kid.

Some people, like Mrs. Donnell, however, are a few bubbles off plumb. She huffed into the principal's office with an earth-shaking complaint. Mr. Laird called me into the meeting. The mother was hot! *Of Mice and Men* has swear words — "damn" and "hell." How can we justify introducing obscenity to our students? She raged, "I read cussing everywhere in that book. It's all trash. Trash."

Using his quiet voice, Mr. Laird explained the school district policy, especially the part stating that she could not censor the book for all students, but she could request a different title for her daughter, Codi. Mrs. Donnell cooled down a little.

I asked her if she'd read the whole story. No. I mentioned that the author's purpose was to point out our human need for family, for roots, for belonging. No response, but I'm nothing if not persistent. I babbled on some more, saying that the kids loved the story, that the language merely fits the types of characters Steinbeck portrayed — itinerant workers.

For some reason, she pulled herself up into battle readiness whenever I talked, but I couldn't seem to shut up. "Do you remember reading Steinbeck in high school — *The Red Pony*, maybe? His stuff is invariably in one anthology or another, he's that good."

No, no she never heard of him, and was mighty glad she hadn't.

The principal interjected, managing to repair my damage and calm her back down. He said we'd take her concern under advisement as a department, that maybe the play version, instead of the novel, would be less offensive. He thanked her for her parental concern, saying how wonderful it was to meet caring parents.

When she finally left, I started back to class, but the assistant principal called us over to his cubicle. "Was that Mrs. Donnell? I should have told her that Codi has two days in school suspension for screaming, 'Shut your fuckin' mouth, you bitch!' to her ex-girlfriend in the lunchroom today."

Codi never read *those* words in Steinbeck.

Guess Steinbeck's occasional "hell" or "damn" was a real bad influence on Codi Donnell, unleashing a whole flash flood of expletives she didn't even know she knew!

Mrs. Donnell, like Mrs. Clamdon and Mrs. Martin, wanted to shield her daughter from the bumps and bruises of the school world — and from me, too. Once I finally got over taking everything parents said personally, I could read between the lines. Their real message was, "I love my growing child, moving away from me at the speed of light." Love brought these moms to school.

KYLE THE CLENCHED FIST

I asked Kyle's mom and dad to come to school. They weren't worried about a few swear words; they were worried about keeping Kyle in school. At fifteen, he was a little young to be out on the streets all day. In class, he was so vitriolic that the rest of the students practically put their hands over their ears when he exploded. As his emotional temperature shot up, his language plummeted into the toilet. I tried to hold onto him, but he practically begged to be kicked out, almost daily.

My conversation with his mom wasn't productive. And often I'd have to oblige Kyle. Every time I called Kyle's mom to let her know what Kyle was, and wasn't, doing, she talked fleetingly about her dead-end problems with him. But then she invariably maneuvered the conversation to focus on herself. I figured the woman needed therapy.

She told me Kyle's story. He'd had brain surgery as an elementary kid, a benign tumor. Never quite the same since. Prone to depression. Been on Prozac since the summer of his eighth-grade year. She'd send him out to empty the garbage and he'd come back, maybe, two days later. He was red, pulsing anger, in and out of school. They'd committed him to the local psych ward twice.

Later the counselor hinted to me that Kyle's father knocked his wife and son around. That helped explain some of the anger issues, but the unsolicited bit of family history didn't help meld him into our classroom home at all. After his parents admitted him into the mental health center in the middle of second semester, he never returned to class. I wrote about Kyle in my teacher journal — tried to sort out the puzzle his life presented to me as a classroom teacher. One thing for sure: his apron strings were choking the life out of him.

Kyle
You keep your hair buzzed
to sport with some defiance
the Z-shaped scar,
evidence of brain surgery you had in fourth grade.
"I'm going to join the Marines," you brag,
"to get out of the house."
I met your mom and dad.
Your mom's face is a carnation;
dad's as tight as a clenched fist.
I hear he uses them on both of you.
Kyle, study your own face in the mirror.
See? Sometimes your smile is more like a grimace too.
Gentleness like your mom's is not gender-specific.

I've lost track of Kyle. He wanted to be a Marine. I hope he found his way there, or some place, where the nature of the work might offer him a balance between his brutality and his bleeding need for a lap of comfort.

REGINA, OUR LADY OF SORROWS

As if adolescence isn't scary enough with all those strange morphing sensations careening around inside the body. To make matters worse, some kids' outer worlds transform, too, often at the speed of light.

Regina's story is not uncommon in our town with F. E. Warren Air Force Base just across the highway from the high school. Military families transfer a lot. Regina's mom just moved from Lompoc, California. Left her dad there. So, besides the adjustment of a move, Regina had a divorce to deal with. Somehow this tough little survivor prevailed, but not without suffering.

I couldn't help noting Regina's emotional roller coaster. Every day a different Regina came in the first period classroom. Sometimes she bounced in, all light and exuberance, her body creating a light breeze, ruffling the loose papers on desks as she skipped by. Like sunflowers, Buddy and Greg, her sidekicks, turned their faces to her beaming light. How to explain such joyful moments? Maybe she awoke filled with her natural hopefulness, the sun casting a friendly beam across her bedspread, the toast in the kitchen smelling like home.

But most days Regina limped across the threshold seconds before the tardy bell. She sagged against the wall like she might throw up or faint. Her skin white as notebook paper, her dark hair and eyes black in contrast. On those days, Greg and Buddy glanced up at her face and then down at their desktops.

Regina wrote of her utter despair, dripping tears on her white notebook paper. She missed her real house in Lompoc. She missed Pepper, her little terrier. Her dad had to keep him since her mom couldn't have a pet in an apartment. Unlike

Lompoc, with no wind, no snow, no brutal cold, the wind here attacked her hair. She missed her boyfriend. As offensive half-back on the varsity football team, a small guy with lightning speed, he was a big shot, and being his girlfriend made her a homecoming star.

Yes, this transplant's roots were shocked in Wyoming's foreign soil. Regina wrote about the bruising moves:

A Silent Protest

My small, child-like protest
is not heard
over my parent's authority.
I am comfortable.
I don't want to uproot
And leave…
again.
Every two years
my life is shoved
into a new state,
a new town
new people.
I am tired,
tired of changes
and tired of not being heard.
I glance around my room
memories
locked in cardboard prisons
ready to be taken away
in a pre-arranged burglary.
I argue

65

scream
and cry.
I am ignored.
No one can hear me
No one cares.
I shut the door.

Clearly, Regina knew why her heart was breaking. All this moving, yanking her roots out over and over. But she cocked her head and half frowned, half smiled as she reread her words, as if seeing them out there in plain sight helped her understand the predicament she was in. I wrote this poem and gave it to Regina. From the looks of her expression, she didn't act like she liked it that much. She sort of shrugged her shoulders, folded up the paper, and stuck it deep in her backpack.

Regina
weeps.
Sorrowing is her business.
A native woman,
she'd cut wounds upon her arm,
her blood, like her eyes, dripping.
A Victorian woman,
she'd wear widow's weeds, all black,
entertaining no visitors.
Inside, she hurts.
Her father left.
She had to move.
She isn't the popular girl in tenth grade here.
How much more proof does she need
that life isn't one long Homecoming parade,
with her the queen?

The next year I occasionally ran into Regina in the halls. Despite everything, there was something indestructible about her. Every time I saw her, she seemed steadier. Then as a senior, she took one of my classes again. Calm maturity radiated from her eyes. She said, in effect, I'm OK now, Mrs. Lain. I'm home, at least inside.

AMBER SEES PERIPHERY

For all of us, bringing up teenagers is a hair-raising experience. One teeth-grinding question we face is how, and when, to let go. We never know if we have the timing right. For Amber's extraordinary parents, the lesson was acute. According to Julie, Amber's best friend, Amber's father was "anal." An intellectual girl, Amber was not a rebellious daughter. It wasn't in her nature to be flamboyant like her friend and writing partner, Julie, who slammed around forcing a fit. Amber sat quietly observing with her keen hazel eyes, eyes whose color matched her name. Today she studies physics in an Ivy League School thousands of miles away from home.

Amber's dad was an engineer by day and a recluse the rest of the time. He and his wife bought a farm 25 miles east of town, and they home-schooled Amber and her sister away from the decadence of the world he worked in every day. When Amber reached her sophomore year, her parents bit the bullet and checked her into the high school so she could take foreign language, calculus, physiology and anatomy. They wanted her to get used to schooling in a non-home setting. They wanted her to have a high school transcript so she could more easily enter a big-name college. But they also wanted to protect her.

I met Amber when she was a senior taking my composition class. Her scholarliness was imposing to her classmates and a pleasure for me. In psych class, Amber learned about Pavlov's operant conditioning and Skinner's notions of programmed instruction. She read about Skinner's famous "baby box," a controlled environmental chamber for infants. Skinner's daughter Deborah spent part of her first two years in the baby box. Somehow, the news struck a chord inside. Amber decided to research two contrasting world views: the behaviorism of B.F. Skinner and a more transformational view like Carl Jung's.

She asked me what she might read to refute the behaviorism model. I remembered my husband's copy of Erich Fromm's *Escape from Freedom*. She borrowed the book and quoted Fromm in her paper: " … man is tempted to surrender his freedom to dictators of all kinds, or to lose it by transforming himself into a small cog in the machine, well fed, well clothed, yet not a free man but an automaton."

Amber loved her parents and her carefully engineered girlhood. But as a senior, her research was a gentle rebellion, breaking out of her baby box. Thinking about Amber's dad, B.F. Skinner and my own strict father, I wrote a little note-poem for her, trying to capture what she taught me. I wondered… maybe Amber's restricted access to the world made her senses more sensitive. During the quiet years, maybe she learned to see even more clearly.

> *Amber*
> *Your strict father*
> *squinted his eyes*
> *and took aim on a narrow view.*
> *Like B.F. Skinner*
> *he tried to put you in a bubble.*
> *But it can't contain you.*
> *Lying there*

you still smell the clover purple fragrance
dissolve into living soil
hear the cells like bees buzzing the breath of life.
You press your nose
against the cool night glass
and ride the shafts of tender moonlight into sleeping
    sagebrush fields
You smell on the wind's breath
spring crouching beneath the snow
gathering green to velvet the earth
Amber,
See?
Even in the bubble
the periphery!

When school let out for summer, Amber and Julie trooped into my room with a bouquet of flowers. "I should be giving you girls flowers. You are the ones graduating." The lovely gesture told me that Amber apprehended my message to her, that she was growing gracefully outward in expanding concentric circles of awareness. And that her father's protectiveness stemmed from love.

LORI'S BRUISES

Like Amber, ninth-grade Lori loved her father. Unlike Amber, Lori and her dad fought. Lori's dad knocked her around once in a while. Lori didn't tell me this; the guidance counselor did.

In spite of the bruising, Lori loved the man. When he was assigned to go to Turkey for six months, she missed him terribly and wrote about the vacant place he left behind. Not long ago, Lori, now an adult, wept over his death. Something about this girl, maybe her queenly manner, tall stature, aloofness, provoked him, mostly when he was drinking.

I didn't give this poem to Lori, just jotted it down after hearing the news that under her white blouse were bruises planted by her dad. Sometimes I just needed to write, like the kids do, to sort myself out, trying to understand the lessons life dished my way.

> *Lori*
> *Tall, elegant*
> *moves through the shorter mass*
> *down the hall*
> *like a gazelle stepping carefully.*
> *Under the clothes are bruises*
> *your father's rage*
> *vents on white skin,*
> *yet unstretched, unused by other men.*
> *Something in your long neck,*
> *your long view down straight nose,*
> *your sure sense of self*
> *drives your father berserk*
> *when he drinks.*
> *The social worker came today and took a photograph of*
> *   blue marks*
> *Now you are down the hall in band*
> *fingers curl expectantly over*
> *silver cool flute*
> *eyes dance the notes across the page*
> *muscles poise to respond.*

Lori and I didn't discuss her dad ever. It felt like a line I shouldn't cross over. No matter, a warm bond developed between the two of us. Three years after I had her in class, a "special teacher" piece came in the school mail. Lori wrote this little reflection of her schooling during her senior year. Her teacher sent me a copy, with Lori's permission.

Special Teacher
A memorable teacher was my ninth grade English teacher.
I was behind in my English class and I had a lot of problems. I don't think she knew about any of them but she made me feel good. She would tell me that I could do it and made me stay after school for days until I finished. I didn't like spending my lunches working but in the end I was pleased. I don't think she remembers or even thinks about me, but I think about her.
Lori

After I got Lori's note, I wrote her back. I mentioned the poem she'd written about lying on the ground, looking up through the bare, skinny arms of a crab apple tree in winter, about how the gray lines were like a message written on the blue sky. I noted how I watched her play flute in a band concert, her whole body a study in attentiveness to the music and the director's baton. Lori didn't know how indelibly her memory remained with me.

Ally Picks Up Pieces

Ally was anything but overprotected by her father. Her mom, a janitor for an insurance company, died in a freak elevator accident, leaving her eldest daughter to take her place: mothering the two younger children, mending the bridges between her older brother estranged from the father, and harnessing her gadabout dad long enough to get him to buy groceries and pay the utilities. A Spartan man, Ally's dad worked seasonal jobs. In the summer, he fought forest fires. In the fall he hired out as a hunting guide. When he was home, he was taciturn, undemonstrative.

A throwback to early trappers, hermits, prospectors, and Nordic sea captains, and maybe a forerunner of future space explorers, he was happiest as far away from people as he could get, standing solitary on a promontory surveying the distance. I've known men like him, for our state is a kind of last frontier. Not a cruel man, he was still unforgiving, especially of his eldest son.

Some student brought a *Life* magazine article to class explaining how Mars could be made inhabitable for humans. "All we need to do is haul up trees to plant and create conditions for an atmosphere," this student explained. Following a class discussion on the possibilities of inhabiting that planet, Ally wrote in her journal an unusually vehement response: "Please, no rocket ship to Mars," and proceeded to elaborate about her dad. She could just picture him, the first to be ready to go, grinching all the time as soon as the place filled up with people.

This is another piece I jotted in my teaching journal but didn't give to Ally. Still, because I wrote about Ally, I understood her better. Though I didn't talk to her directly about "problems," I sort of put my compassion out there in the air hoping she could read it somehow.

Ally
Your clenchjawed father's heavy booted departure
pushes the family to the brink again
of Ice Age.
In his avalanche of greed to conquer the peaks

he heads out for higher ground.
His dilated eyes survey the panorama below.
He leaves you and the kids to patch up the tent after the
    snowfall.
You huddle
trading fat cells to live.
His brainstem lacks
what women know
of chinking between the logs
and red calico curtains on the frost-encrusted window
The earth needs
a woman's view to seal the cracks
against howling wind
to embrace Cain home without a beating
to carry fresh-baked bread down the road to the
    neighbors.
I agree with you when you say, "Please, I don't need no
    rocket thrust to Mars."

73

Ally grew up and moved to Denver. She started as a bank teller and now is the office manager in the loan department, supervising a whole room full of people. She hasn't married, yet.

ANNAMARIE THE BELOVED

Many of my students enjoy an uncomplicated, warm relationship with their parents in spite of the roller coaster years. AnnaMarie was no exception. Hers was a most nurturing father who tried and succeeded in raising his kids single-handedly. He took AnnaMarie to buy her prom dress, comforted her when she broke up with Jason. My poem to AnnaMarie validated this lovely bond between father and daughter, how from child-hood on, he'd tried to break her every fall, an impossible task as she moved into adulthood. I'll bet her warm memories of her father will comfort her all her life.

> *AnnaMarie*
> *A bright blue helium balloon escaped*
> *from your hand clutched somewhere*
> *on Saturday*
> *I glimpsed its escape from my window*
> *in your journal*
> *sailing against rooftops*
> *free*
> *I see the round ohhhs escape*
> *from your sad mouth*
> *as chin uptilted*
> *your eyes race to keep up with the fleeing*
> *tears rush rivulets into your hair*
> *the nagging sorrow of something lost.*
> *Your father is helpless*
> *to retrieve it*
> *fists clenched*
> *He can't leap up and capture your bright blue promises.*

In my mind's eye, AnnaMarie's father is there, standing right beside her as she sits in her desk in my room.

Families always accompany the kids to school, whether vis-ible or invisible. It makes for a crowded room. If I choose to teach, ignoring their presence, I kid myself. The students bring their families to school, and that's where they belong, for to really learn, these students need to weave what I teach into the already existing patterns of their lives, including their family ties. The apron strings do get tangled, but I have to work with parents to really teach their kids. The writing I did for myself in my journal, as well as the poems I gave to the students, helped me sort out and understand the complexities when parents and families come to school.

Meanwhile, I hold in my hands two sets of apron strings — those tying me to my home and those connecting me to all my students.

CHAPTER FIVE

Learning Styles

GREW up school-smart. From first grade on, I loved school, except for occasional dry spells like fifth grade, the worksheet year, or seventh grade, the year of the dorky anthology with stories I couldn't put together into any kind of pattern. School loved me, too, most of the time. In first grade Mrs. Shabbot kissed me goodbye before Dad whisked me away for Christmas at Grandma's house, a long, long ways away. High school teachers like Mr. Aquilar and Miss Biddle came to see me and hug me when I was hospitalized after a near-fatal car wreck.

Now, I wasn't the very smartest one in my class. Carol was. And I wasn't equally smart in all subjects. But seldom did I suffer a bruised ego in school for not measuring up. I thought everybody learned pretty much the way I did, remembering little facts for multiple choice tests and memorizing multiplication tables. That's what I thought until I got married.

My husband looks at the world with entirely different eyes. We went through college together. Sometimes we even took the same class. On the astronomy final, for example, he'd get a C and I'd get an A. Then I'd forget all the material the moment I crossed the threshold on my way out the door. Gayle, on the other hand, *still* remembers all the names of all the planets, the constellations, the theories and the theorists.

We were debate partners in college. Here I'd be, scribbling down all the minute details of the first affirmative speaker and scrabbling through the card file finding rebuttal arguments. Meanwhile, Gayle would lean back, arms folded across his chest, and see right to the heart of the argument, pinning down the underlying flaw. When we won debates, it was because of the way he saw the big picture.

But he *cannot* spell. He doesn't spell the same word the same way ... ever! Or so it seems. I think if there'd been special education back in 1947 when he was in first grade, he'd have been labeled "disabled in written expression." He'd be pulled out and drilled on spelling words and rules until the poor teacher would pull her hair out. He *wasn't* labeled, but he *was* the first one down in every spelling bee. One kindly teacher told him, "Don't worry, Gayle. Someday you'll have a secretary to fix your spelling." She was right. Since those spelling bee years, he's written a doctoral dissertation, published a Wyoming history book, and written a novel, with, admittedly, a lot of help from spell checks and secretaries.

I watched this foreign-brained person I'd married and thought, "Hmmm. Braininess, the way school measures it, isn't the last word on intelligence."

When we had children, I learned even more about the various ways people learn. My daughter, Shan, for example, always looks sideways or backwards at things. She traveled to China in 1988, the year before the uprising in Tiananmen Square. She went with the People to People program. One early morning, the American students crawled out of bed to see a tourist attraction—the sunrise from the tallest pagoda in Beijing. Shan admired the sun coloring the eastern sky for a few moments, but then she turned around to look behind her.

From her high vantage point, she could look down into dozens of tiny yards, eight-by-eight-foot enclosures visually blocked from the others by fences. As if they were choreographed, men, dressed in what she thought were identical pajama bottoms, emerged from their houses, yawned and stretched, and commenced to lift their arms and legs, one at a time, in rhythm with the ascending sun, unconsciously in sync with each other. She was so moved that she stood transfixed until Alan, a fellow traveler, poked her to awareness. "What are you doing, Shan?" And he, too, turned and witnessed the dance.

When she got home, she told me, "Mom, every single man thought he was dancing alone, but he was really part of a huge ensemble...and they didn't even know it!"

Shan learned a lot by looking backward off that pagoda. My family and my students have taught me a lot about learning. How unique we all are, how some people look from the other side, how some can't learn the little pieces until they can apprehend the whole. Now, I'm hard pressed to say one person is smart and another is dumb. Some people like Shan look in different directions; some like Gayle look to the heart of the matter and skip the details. It all depends. One way isn't better than another.

Weldon's Writing Sings

"You're the first person who believed in me." Weldon said this years after I'd had him in class. I'd found his writing, albeit misspelled and ungrammatical, breathtakingly clear, fresh as spring asparagus shooting up along the irrigation ditch banks. He was starved for affirmation, for a star here and there in his writing, a ☆ meaning, "This is awesome!"

Weldon's dad was a dairy farmer. Technology helps relieve the workload of a dairy only a little. Those cows, and their huge burdens of milk swaying between back legs, require plenty of attention — the morning and night rituals, rounding them up, moving them gently into their stalls, setting the pumps to their teats. The cows' complex equipment needs repair as often as the milking machines.

I took one look at Weldon, his sandy, straight hair slanting across that wide forehead, his shy, bucktoothed grin, humble and self-effacing, his fingers as thick around as a hoe handle, and I remembered my own sweet-natured uncle George, long dead, who milked Jerseys for forty years. There's something about people who make a living around milk cows; they are patient and cooperative like the animals they tend.

Weldon never had a real girlfriend, but he was sweet on Rachel whose folks had a ranch twenty miles north. He had a favorite class, wood shop, and a least favorite, English. I didn't give Weldon the following poem, wrote it years after I had him in class. He triggered the memories when he called me long distance the other day, asking, "Do you remember me?"

Hey, Weldon!
I see you there,
ears drooping over an open book
unable to meet your teacher's pale blue eyes
cold as judgment
You can't define her past participle
or discern the implications of the subjunctive — from

the worksheet.
At your locker,
you and the other heavy-footed boys,
heads shorn like spring sheep,
grin toothy,
hunch shoulders,
dip heads,
define embarrassment.
In the middle of the direct nominatives,
you wander off
thinking
of blond wood shavings
thin as a girl's ribbon of hair
curling tenderly around your thick finger.
Stubbed nails
scrubbed
hands dry
exposed to daily winter pitch forks
and milk bucket handles
you dream of wood
shaped into curved cabinets
satin finish smooth as a girl's lips.

Today Weldon works for the State Conservation Service. His wife is a teacher and a published romance novelist. He writes some, too, mostly publishing over the Internet.

LOUIE WORKS FROM WHOLE TO PARTS

Louie was a similar case, only I taught him more recently. I got to know him in my high school composition class, an elective listed in the registration book as essential for collegebounders. He fully expected to get, maybe, a D. The reason he didn't have higher aspirations is because he had been tested in first grade and put in special ed. His disability was written language. He said he usually avoided *hard* English classes.

The first half of the semester called for essay writing. Louie kept up fine with plenty of coaching from me and from his peer writing group, but when research-paper time rolled around, he got antsy. The weight was so heavy on this part of the curriculum that he was pretty nervous. Besides, the research paper was a long-term project requiring lots of reading and, woe to Louie, lots of writing. The closer we got to the start of the research project, the more his legs danced under his desk.

The first day of the unit, I led the kids through a self-inventory so they could think of a topic to research — one they'd really like. I asked questions aloud and they wrote their responses in their journals. Louie loosened up a bit as he scribbled. He listed his favorite movies and paused to think about what they might have in common. He skipped over the questions about his religious beliefs — which was fine because everyone didn't have to answer every question — but he got into explaining the gist of the last good discussion around the dinner table with his family — whether Hopkinson, a local killer, should get the death penalty. The whole period spun away, very few kids checking the time, while Louie and his classmates answered questions about their interests, their dreams for the future, and the big ideas they ponder.

After a few days of such self-searching activities and with some coaching and talking, both with me and his group, Louie decided to do his research on learning disabilities. In the process he learned about Howard Gardner, a scholar who explained the various ways people learn. Some of us might learn better through words while others might learn through physical activities.

By the time our class actually started researching, Louie settled down and his legs quit jiggling.

Once the paper was written, the students were to present their project orally in front of the class. This presentation needed to get all of us actively involved. "Show us, don't just tell us," I told the students. So Louie decided to bring in his fly-tying rig, the one he started when he was eight years old.

He showed us all kinds of flies and mosquitoes — Royal Coachman, the prettiest of all. Deftly he tied several for us as a demonstration. Then, breaking us into groups, he had us go at it. He coached even the most fumble-fingered to tie our own flies. Louie talked during and after his demo about how people are all different with different types of learning modes, and how he learns best by using his hands. He always knew he was good with his hands, he said, because he did more than tie flies. He helped his dad as a carpenter's helper. His dad's crews were building the new city/county health building.

In his own words, he told us about how hoppin' frustrated he was in school, filling out worksheets that never made sense to him. Heck, he didn't learn to read until fourth grade when finally he got enough of the *whole* reading idea to be able to make use of the bits and parts. He told about remedial classes where, instead of going at the reading from a different tack, his teacher just slowed down, using the same old worksheets and yelling a little louder, like he was deaf. He told us we should just see those check sheets his teacher had to test him on — a list of little bitty skills as long as your arm: capitalize your name, capitalize the names of cities, states, capitalize the names of languages, and on and on.

83

"Heck. We never got to read and write that much. Never got into a discussion."

But now as a senior, Louie wanted a chance to at least try college, so he signed up for this writing class, just to test the water. "Now, even if I'm worried as hell if I'll even pass, I'm glad. I found out I'm not a freak, just a 'tactile learner,' according to this Gardner dude, who's s'posed to know, being's he's from Harvard and all." Besides, Louie went on, he found *Black Elk Speaks*. "I love that book." In his study he showed how, in his opinion, Black Elk was a pretty unusual thinker himself. "See, he was this Native American dude who predicted the future and saw visions, like of the topography of the land from an airplane view — and airplanes hadn't been invented yet!"

After Louie's depiction of his book, several kids checked it out to read.

The poem I gave to Louie paraphrased a story he told about his junior high English class.

> *Louie*
> *you're so mad you spit.*
> *"Basic skills?*
> *I'd say it's basic to want to live first*
> *before learning predicate nominatives,*
> *whatever the hell that is.*
> *Put life on your damn check sheets!"*
> *Knowing how to put commas around*
> *, however,*
> *befuddles you.*
> *On your Black Elk magic carpet ride,*
> *you see wholes in circles first*
> *long before the pieces and parts fit together to make*

sense.

"No one reads the world that straight-line way anyway.
Which one of us is retarded—
the one who fits the outside puzzle pieces together
around the big circle of meaning first?
Or the one who works from inside the puzzle out?"
You walk away utterly pissed off.

CHRISTY THE GOLDEN GIRL

While Weldon and Louie trudged along the muddy road of school, pulling their feet out of one sticky hole after another, Christy breezed along, seemingly effortlessly.

Christy talked for a few minutes about a story she was assigned to teach us, "Boys and Girls." In it, author Alice Munro is peeved. Growing up on a Canadian wheat farm meant lots of work, but her brother got to work outside while she was relegated to odious kitchen duties.

Christy wanted to talk about gender bias, gender issues. So she baked cookies. Using a generic gingerbread cookie cutter, she cut out one cookie for each kid. Then she grouped us into fours, gave each group four containers with four colors of icing and asked that we decorate the cookies. We'd be able to eat the cookies at the end of class, but first we were to decorate.

Off we went, coloring. Some kids mixed colors. Some planned. Some smeared. Meanwhile Christy set up a display table with numbered empty spots, presumably where the cookies would be positioned. When time was up for the decorating, Christy collected the cookies and put each on the table beside a number. Then she had us write the numbers from 1 through 24 in our spirals. We had 24 students in the room. We got up and began to write down B for boy or G for girl beside each number, depending upon whether we thought that the decorator was male or female. She wondered if we had predispositions about what a boy's cookie would look like. Christy had us grade our gender tests. Were we able, based upon the colors, the neatness or lack of neatness, the types of patterns, to discern which cookies were decorated by boys and which by girls? She wondered, is there such a thing as gender difference? We found out we couldn't discern gender by merely looking at how cookies were decorated. She had kids reflect in their journals on gender bias in their own lives while we ate our cookies. The whole lesson was yummy.

When it came to school, Christy had no rough edges. She loved to read and write, do math and science. To top it all off, she loved to work.

Christy
Caribbean blondness like white sand
and blue sky sea eyes
masks a steely will
to sell the most candy in the world
to be first in French
win science fairs
writing contests.
You take all the time necessary to achieve perfection.
You'll walk on through every hallway,
skirting detours
and finish each race with pride.
I see your sheepskin hanging there
beside the Hippocratic oath,
Dr. Adolphson.

GUILLERMO FLIES

Long after Guillermo graduated, I wrote this piece, a sort of personal reflection about life's ironies. Mrs. Blevins was our school nurse in the country school where I first taught. Some people called her the Iron Maiden, but not to her face. She hauled kids with head lice to the deep sink in the corner of her office, and the strong-smelling stuff, plus elbow grease, severely reduced the little critters' chances for survival. When teachers complained to her that so-and-so had serious body odor, she showered the little stinkers. If she had to, she got into the shower fully dressed in her white dress and sensible shoes to give them the scrubbing they never got at home. We car pooled together; I paid her for the privilege of riding in her 1959 green Biscayne Chevrolet. I had two little kids to get ready in the morning and sometimes she had to wait a few minutes. To break me of the habit, once she drove to school extra slow, making me late for first period. I hadn't noticed because I always graded papers during the forty-minute drive. The principal was not pleased that my first-hour class was unattended for ten minutes.

Inside that refrigerator-shaped body and straight-line mind of hers, Mrs. Blevins was kind. One summer she took advanced nursing classes in Los Angeles, some special program. She stayed with her sister, a social worker. One thing led to another and Blevins came home with a juvenile delinquent to finish raising. I had Guillermo in class and followed his life after high school. This poem was not for him to read, but it helped me think about learners, all of whom are seeking to find a balance between the way they learn and the demands the world places on them.

Guillermo
At school Mrs. Blevins said she rescued your brown-
    skinned ass
from the California Penitentiary for Youth
and a life of drugs and crime.
It was a spur-of-the-moment thing,
an uncharacteristic right-brained thing to do,
she from eastern Wyoming near the Nebraska line,
her white bread view
flat as a cornfield
no taste for hot picante.
You came because maybe Wyoming
was a better sentence
than three years in jail.
From pimples you became clear skinned
donned a button shirt and tie
for graduation.
Kissed it good-bye to go back
give the old life another try
She was stung by the rejection.
After a year retasting PCP and floating in a fog,
you called again
said you'd enlisted in the army
four years
you'd go her way
rules comfortably tight.
Ha!
Now
you're a paratrooper
jumping into the sky
adrenaline singing joy in your veins

as close as you can get to balance
her way and yours
left brained and right
flying as best you can, not being a bird.

If there is any evidence that the right and left brain di-chotomy truly exists, Guillermo's way of thinking was right-brained. He wasn't on friendly terms with his bossy, linear mind at all. He daydreamed, remembered lyrics to songs, rode the skateboard so automatically he could be asleep. Mrs. Blevins tried, but she couldn't yank Guillermo's perception of the world around to match her own.

89

CHERYN READS WITH HER HANDS

Once in a while, in the middle of a writing project or after a silent reading time, I'd break out the art supplies. Making visual representations of ideas in reading and writing were a lifeline for Cheryn, a sophomore who learned through her hands. One day, I asked the students to create collages to use as book talks. Scissors, glue, markers and magazines were every-where. Cheryn stopped dead still at the doorway. "Ohhhh, it smells like kindergarten in here!" Her face transformed. The glazed eyes turned bright, like a switch went on in her head. The whole period was yellow sunshine.

Cheryn created a nifty one-page drawing, a visual meta-phor of her free-choice novel, *The House on Mango Street* by Sandra Cisneros. Little excerpts of the book were in our five-pound anthology, but these snippets had done nothing for Cheryn. She couldn't hear the voice, sense the purpose of the work. I showed her my copy of the Cisneros book and read her a little. She eyed the slimness of the volume and decided to borrow it. Though she didn't enjoy the snippets in the anthology, she did enjoy the little paperback. Each vignette drew a picture inside Cheryn's head. During the art project, she picked up a piece of brown construction paper and a piece of white. Her scissors flew; we only had one 44-minute period to create the book reports and share them, time being the most precious commodity in secondary school. She cut the two pieces of paper into the shape of a tenement building, and cut windows in the brown one, little windows that were hinged on one side and opened and closed. She glued the white and brown paper together. Inside each window, on the white paper, she glued or drew little scenes — one was a gray-haired lady arranging flowers — she cut that photo out of *Modern Maturity* magazine. Her finished work resembled those Christmas calendars for children, the ones with the windows that open up. Out in front of the tenement, Cheryn glued one scrawny little tree.

On the back of her visual, Cheryn wrote two lines: "Her name was Esperanza — Hope. Her hope was growing up and finding a better house, but, like this tree, she didn't want to forget her roots."

Cheryn loved the visual metaphor-making. She took over these occasions, setting up supplies, walking around the room coaching her classmates, hanging up the work around the room, and cleaning up afterward. I wrote to her.

Cheryn
everyday
early
you poke
around the corner
to see what errands to run

what tasks to perform before the bell.
It brightens my day to see you
brown-eyed, brown-skinned beauty
with a great black cloud of curling hair.
If I teach only writing straight prose
and taking little round circle tests with #2 pencils
only a tiny part of your beauty shows
glistens
shines.
But if you speak,
draw,
make children's stories,
you, Cheryn, are an A girl.

Cheryn noticed that I valued her unique way of learning.

Mrs. Lain
I like that you don't think I'm a slow brainer.
Cheryn

Once in a while, even in high school, students need to get their hands dirty messing with metaphor. The exercise enriches the thin topsoil of class. Getting at learning from different angles helps students like Cheryn who learn by creating.

CAL QUIT ME

Even with my struggling high school readers, I try to move beyond fill-in-the-blank study guides, but some students won't let me. I get sick of questions like: Who was the main character? Where did the story take place? But Cal loved those simple, black-and-white questions. Then he could do what he always did when he "read." He could hunt and peck his way through a book, figuring if he could answer some of the easy-to-find facts, he could at least pass. But I wanted to get into questions like: Why did William Golding pick the choir boys to be the ones marching together and blindly following the leader until they committed murder? When I asked "Why?" Cal dropped his notebook on the floor. He threw a fit. "Just ask facts. That's what I'm used to." His mantra was, "Why ask why?"

Cal thought reading was a dorky pastime anyway. Poor Cal was caught in a conundrum: he insisted I keep things simple, and then he said he hated English because it was stupid, unimportant to real-life concerns. But he did understand baseball. He was a first-rate shortstop for the American Legion baseball team. Those rules he could understand. I gave him this poem a few weeks before he disappeared from my roster.

> Cal
> Furious
> the spelling and grammar rules so slippery.
> Just makes it hard to win the game.
> "Show me the simple answers," he glares.
> "I'm in new territory here. Just tell me the right rules of
>   this damned class so I can win.
> Draw the lines clear so I can hit this curve ball
> and be safe on first."

With Cal, no matter what, nothing penetrated. School was just collecting Carnegie Units, like picking up bread crumbs *Hansel and Gretel* style, wearily climbing the steps one at a time until graduation. Learning had no attachment to his life. I tried extra hard for Cal. While everyone else was deep into background reading for their literary criticism papers, I started reading aloud to him a book I hoped he'd finish, *A Hero Ain't Nothin' But a Sandwich.* If he'd just get through one book, all the way, I thought, maybe he'd get the hang of reading on his own.

He didn't. Cal dropped out. I never got my copy of *Hero* back either. I hope he read it, but I can picture him throwing it in the garbage can out in the hall.

I READ IN THE WOMB

Unlike Cal, I always loved to read. As a kid I read the toothpaste box while I was brushing my teeth. I can't remember when I didn't read. Smuggling books under the covers at night. Feigning homework assignments so I could read *Bobbsey Twins* instead of setting the table. Reading in the car until I was carsick. All the usual childhood read-aholic behaviors.

So when I became an English teacher in 1968 with a room full of kids wildly different in every way, including their reading abilities, I was boggled, defensive, even resentful. After all, shouldn't they be able to read by the time they get to high school? After all, didn't I decide to be an English teacher because I loved literature? I felt like my friend Bab who teaches eighth-grade English. "I've read since I was born. Haven't a clue HOW I learned to read. How am I supposed to teach these big lugs how?"

Now I know my students *can* read — that is, they can decode, or sound out, words. What these kids can't do very well is read for meaning, especially with more difficult texts. It's as if they aren't very good at juggling, and reading is a juggling act. A good reader has to perform various mental tricks at once — noting patterns, hearing the author's voice in their heads, wondering, hypothesizing, recalling memories, and comparing their own versions of life with the author's. This last is very important; I'm convinced that most of my mud-sluggish readers like Cal don't know that the main character in any book is really the reader.

Sorry, Cal, in my room we'll continue to connect the books to our lives. So before we crack open the book *To Kill a Mockingbird*, we'll write about powerful childhood memories. Or we'll try to write like the author. I've seen more "ah-hah" looks when I've asked kids to imitate the author's style. The kids have their journals right there, open, every day, so it's easy to slip into a writing mode. I ask students to use the reading journal as a place to think through their reading. Question. Sneer. Argue. Agree. I like a reading journal much more than a fill-in-the-blanks study guide. Reading is so much more than filling in the blanks.

Though Cal quit, he taught me to figure out more strategies to teach reading. Lots of my students in high school are pretty reluctant readers — even J.C., who was heading to the Air Force Academy, didn't read for pleasure, which meant he didn't read very much at all.

One teaching strategy that works for me is reading aloud. I started reading *Fahrenheit 451* aloud to the kids — thought they'd be more fluent on their own if they could just get into the rhythm of Bradbury's prose, could hear his voice, how he put words and sentences together. As I read, I realized some of the kids' foreheads were furrowing. These ultra-literals weren't getting Bradbury's figurative language. So I began to model how to understand the words by reading out loud and then saying, in *sotto voce,* what my "other" mind was wondering as I read.

"It was a pleasure to burn." *Mmmm. I used to like to burn stuff. Play with matches.*

94

"It was a special pleasure to see things eaten, to see things blackened and changed." *Ouch. What the heck is he talking about. I thought we were talking about "burned" and now he's saying "eaten." Oh. Well I guess fire sorta eats.*

"With the brass nozzle in his fists, with this great python spitting its venomous kerosene upon the world, ... " *Oh, for crying out loud. What's the brass nozzle? What's the great python? Could this be the hose, maybe? Yeah, a hose is like a python. Venomous? I didn't know pythons have venom. Well, I guess some snakes are poisonous. This author is going to make me work. Uses lots of metaphors, crazy verbs.*

"With his symbolic helmet numbered 451 on his stolid head, and his eyes all orange flame ... ." *How can his eyes be orange?*

" ... he flicked the igniter and the house jumped up in a gorging fire that burned the evening sky red." *What? How can a house jump up? How can a fire burn the evening sky red?*

Yes, Bradbury's language throws some of these reading bloodhounds off the trail. Not very motivated anyway, they lose the scent and circle around, diffidently sniffing the ground. But even if the book doesn't appeal to everyone, even though some very literal students can't begin to follow Bradbury's rich prose, even though the first lines give those left-brainers a splitting headache, we read on with me thinking out loud, showing the students how my mind makes sense — by wondering, backtracking and connecting.

SAM THE HAMMER MAN

Sam was a Cal, transformed. Once he caught on to reading for a purpose — like to help him argue wildly in class and to write cool prose — he read. He devoured all of Bradbury's books as an extension of *Fahrenheit 451*. I caught the whiff of Bradbury between the lines of Sam's writing. Talk about the power of imitation! His metaphors tasted good, pleased the eye. His verbs shimmered. He created a feeling of nostalgia, writing about summers fishing with his dad. His parents were divorced.

Sam wrote: "Summer was one long sigh. My arms part of the fishing line, my fingers sensing the nose of a fish down, down under the mirror." His writing blew me away. He continued gulping down books that year in his sophomore English class. Later, he wrote me at Christmas from college. He said he was reading.

I remember once reading that maybe inmates in prison have too many Y chromosomes — the ones that make them prone to acting out. Sam might have had an extra Y chromosome or Attention Deficit Disorder or both. He could *not* sit still. Here he was — a shoe-in for a college football scholarship, the hammer man at forward, feared by everyone he guarded, and state champion high hurdler. But he made more enemies than he could apologize to, if he cared to apologize, which he didn't. He pushed people too hard. He got kicked out of class because he'd suddenly become an arm-swinging maniac; he got kicked off the basketball team his senior year because he got in a fight with the starting guard, the head coach's pet.

I gave him this poem.

Sam
Arms, windmills.
Mouth, barnyard, zoo, car crash.
Energy.
You push the boundaries of propriety
with "school inappropriate language."

After you read every one of his books,
you wrote like Ray Bradbury.
Your dad lives inside tattooed skin
and blows up
in a Harley
belly and all.
You live with your mom who pays the bills.
Sam the Hammer Man.
At Burger Inn, one of your three jobs
around ball practice and a 3.3 GPA,
you run, don't walk, to the dumpsters and
clean like a wind-up toy on high speed.
You know, with all the things that could go wrong—
undiagnosed Attention Deficit Disorder
and alcohol imprinted on your father's breath—
you went right.
Go figure, Despair.

I was proud of Sam, of the whole human race because of the living proof of him. I even liked his rough edges — chicken squawks and all — in the back of my English class. I think he liked me too. Sam came by the house on graduation day. He'd sort of become extended family because he worked for one of my sons. He hugged me a little — sort of an off-to-the-side hug.

ANDAN

Andan the Motormouth was a challenge. Talked all the time. Even backtalked to his mom. (I'd heard snatches of a phone conversation home.) She was probably trying to get him to focus and be responsible and shut up, for God's sake, once in a while.

Nothing worked.

But Andan was a marvelous teacher. He made good connections. His class presentation for the research project was priceless. At first, we had a little wrestling match over the topic-versus-thesis issue. He insisted he wanted to write about baseball in Babe Ruth's day. I insisted that the paper had to be more than a report — it had to be a thesis paper. "What's a thesis, anyway?" he asked me about two hundred times and never listened. He finally caught on when I said, "It's just a report with an attitude." So, finally, his thesis claimed that baseball in the '40s and '50s was more authentic than it is today: the players weren't paid so well, the game wasn't a big business racket for the owners and organizers, and the teams traveled all over the country playing with ordinary people in every little hamlet, making baseball synonymous with apple pie and America.

Then for Andan's oral presentation, he brought in a huge collection, a museum really, of baseball mitts thirty, forty, fifty years old. He explained how these were made, what they were made to do, how they compare with gloves today. Kids handled them lovingly, sniffing the leather and thinking about summer sun and green diamonds.

Andan
Motormouth
idling front row center
revving up the engine slightly now and then
to match the rise and fall of my voice.
I heard you talk like a barking hyena to your mom, too.
Comforting to know you don't reserve disrespect
just for me.
Hippopotami yawn complete with sound effects.

You watch every single opportunity to be center stage,
girls giggling.
You need the heavy hand of Authority pushing your face
to the pavement
every single second.

Andan's response to me was generous. Even after I lambasted him for talking all the time, he bounced right back with a huge grin and a gentle cuff on my arm.

My whole family and my students teach me a lot about teaching. I'm hard pressed to say one person like Christy is "smart" and one like Weldon is "dumb." Some people simply look in different directions, like my daughter, Shan. Some, like Gayle, look to the heart of the matter and skip all the details. Everyone in my classroom is different, and one way of learning isn't better than another. My job is to watch these people closely and match what I say to the ways they can hear best.

CHAPTER SIX

Strange Students in a Strange Land

JUNIOR highs house lunatics, and I don't mean just the students.

I'd taught four years in high school before we moved from central Wyoming to Cheyenne. In our new home town, I landed a junior high teaching job, and thus began a stint of some fifteen years with the nose-picking crowd who taught me about rocking along, afloat on a sea of hormones.

The first faculty meeting should have warned me. The teachers at the table across from mine giggled maniacally while the principal talked. Their junior high behavior hinted at things to come, a craziness that was confirmed at the first faculty party.

When I came home from the October ice breaker, Gayle asked, "How'd it go?"

"You gotta get me out of this place."

"Why? What happened?"

"Those people threw food at each other. A slice of bologna landed on my head. We were kicked out of the Coors Hospitality Room after the fist fight."

"A fist fight? You gotta be kidding."

"Nope. Ever heard of the horn trick?"

"Oh, yeah. The one where some fool blows flour all over himself?"

"Yeah. The PE guy did it to the music guy. The music guy has good lungs, being a singer and all, and he blew hard on some crazy-looking horn. Didn't realize that the end of the horn was loaded with flour aimed right at his face. He didn't think the prank was funny. He hit the PE guy before those nuts could quit laughing long enough to grab his arms."

Gayle grinned in spite of himself.

"So much stuff was going on I got a headache."

In spite of my culture shock, I didn't resign from that junior high, and by the Christmas faculty party, bologna throwing didn't seem out of the ordinary any more.

Something happens to all the inmates in junior high. The students lead the way, and the teachers follow. The teachers who cut up, resembling their own students, are in some way validating the kids' stages. I've known teachers who perform pratfalls, just to show students they can live through embarrassment. "See, kids," the teacher behavior seems to say, "you fall down, you laugh, you live to tell about it."

During my long stay in junior high, I knew some loonie birds, and some kids filled to the brim with rage, pain, fear. Students this age are like fresh garden tomatoes: they have very thin skins. From them, I learned to dislodge some of my own stuffy perceptions about propriety so I could be a better teacher.

I'm convinced that once I learned to deal with weird people, I really learned to teach.

ROBBIE THE RED BARON

Take seventh-grade Robbie. He was a very strange boy. During finals, he entertained himself, at the same time he was doing a first-rate job of revising a piece for his writing folder, by flying his desk. First, he'd tip the wings to the left. Then he'd tip the wings to the right. He accompanied the maneuvers with sound effects, not too loud, but loud enough for me to hear. When I gave him the teacher-laser look, he winked at me.

Another time, all of us, teacher and students, were right there with Pony Boy in *The Outsider*. Back in our world, a police siren sounded out on Pershing Street. Some of us were so engrossed in escaping the burning building we didn't even register the noise, but Robbie hit the floor shouting, "Take shelter! Take shelter!" He never really quit acting.

Robbie fit into the loonie category. I gave him this poem.

Robbie
So much depends upon
the bright green gum bubble
Robbie blows.
It pops on his nose
a light bright note in this gray day.

My poem to Rob tried to tell him that, for all his kooky behaviors, I liked him. In my words, he could sense that it was OK to be zany. Even grownups need to keep alive some adolescent whackiness — belly laughing, racing their own kids, and retaining a mischievous twinkle in their eyes. Adulthood without a little adolescent goofiness is like 7-Up without carbonation. I wanted Rob to know that I knew he'd grow up. When he did, I had complete confidence he'd remember to zip up his mouth in business meetings.

SCHOOL SUBTRACTS STEVE

While the junior high milieu may be the source of oddball humor, it is also an environment that generates a lot of pain. Steve's ninth-grade year was terrible. Small for his age, Steve prayed to the puberty god for growth. "Please," he'd beg, "let me grow out of size-ten T-shirts." His prayers weren't immediately answered. PE was agony, showering with the other boys, fearing the ridicule he came to expect.

Steve's clenched jaw revealed his barely controlled rage. At school, he held himself rigidly in check. At home, his mom eventually told me, he let it all out, venting. He screamed himself hoarse, even shoved her once, hard. She'd had it, put him in the psych ward of the local hospital for three weeks. After all, she was tired, raising Steve alone with no father to offer support and occasional relief.

At first I didn't know why he disappeared from school. I asked around the lounge. Fran, a science teacher, was there; she didn't know him. Neither did some guy at the coffee machine, whose name I didn't know. No one did. Our school housed about 1,200 students, not large by some standards, but I caught myself feeling that old frustration: this school does more to keep people separated than it does to help us connect. What Native American tribe was it, I mused, that maintained itself at about fifty people? If they exceeded fifty, they couldn't keep track of everyone so the tribe would split.

After the third day, a homebound teacher came to my door, asking for Steve's homework; that's when I learned where he was.

Steve came back to class subdued. He never wrote or talked about the time-out. We both knew where he'd been, but he shut his mouth about the whole experience. I felt sorry for him. He reminded me of my own son, now away in college. Jade used to be a little like Steve. But my boy's rage turned inward, forming a murky pool of depression. At home I talked about Steve, expressing my concern for him. The talk, the fact that a teacher cared, comforted my grown boy, who still remembered the nightmare of adolescence.

I wrote about Steve in my teacher journal.

Steve
does not know
he sits at my dinner table.
I think of him daily and my other blood son
away at college
I know their inner staggerings against walls
and the bruises.
My own son in his long purgatory
cried,
"Is it worth it?
Where's the pattern that makes sense?"
Somehow,
knowing I carry this student around in my heart
comforts my own son.

I hoped that Steve could sense my compassion. I think he did. Three years later I worked with him and 150 other student writers in a writing clinic out at the college. He came up to me and, reserved as he was, touched my arm, a Steve embrace, distant but warm.

Steve wrote about his feelings toward school in a poignant poem about learning the hard way how school subtracts a person.

> *Arithmetic of School*
> *Take the total of a person*
> *Subtract 20% for a parent's degrading remarks.*
> *You are 80%*
> *Subtract another 20% for kids who hinder and pester.*
> *You are 60%*
> *Subtract another 20% for teachers*
> *who do not see, do not help.*
> *You are now 40%.*
> *Lose another 20% a day for relatives*
> *who do not openly love and cherish.*
> *You are 20%.*
> *Drop another 20% due to shyness and low self-esteem.*
> *You are 0.*

Though Steve never openly talked about his "mental" problems, *Arithmetic* communicated his suffering and loneliness. Eventually, he felt strong enough to publish his poem in the school literary magazine.

About School

Whoever thought it would be a good idea to pack goofballs like Robbie and Steve the Sufferer together?

The whole time I worked with this age group, I found myself wishing for something better. A better way to get the job done. Students like Robbie need stages and spotlights and a real audience to play to. For every play in the curriculum, they need to perform in one, complete with spotlights, make-up. They need to connect with someone else in biographies and history books, someone whom they admired, someone who made them cry. For every novel they read raising issues of social class or prejudice, they need to build a bus shelter or deliver a meal on wheels. For every poem to read, they need to write ten and produce literary magazines. They needed newspapers to publish, debates to hold on earth-shaking issues, lots of writing about their lives, their loved ones, their beloved places. And in the process of learning and doing, the sad ones like Steve might feel more at home.

These pseudo-adults needed to stretch their wings, however silly and awkward they look — to take risks and laugh at their own mistakes. Junior highs should be safe places to practice flying, and flopping. Hard to do in the current setting.

I taught fifteen years in a traditional junior high, straight out of the '50s. Fonzie would have felt at home there. Seventh, eighth, and ninth graders careened through the doors at 7:30 A.M., three hours before they were fully awake. They were released at 2:30, three hours before parents came home from work to keep them out of trouble. Lunch lasted twenty minutes — long enough for all of us to wolf down our food, but not long enough for anyone to start a full-fledged food or fist fight.

The bells rang every 44 minutes all day and the lockers were off limits, period, the better to prevent locker horseplay, such as locking small Steve inside. Kids took English, social studies, science, math, P.E., shop, home ec, foreign language, art, music — all segregated from one another, all content-driven.

If you were smart or had aggressive parents, you might land in honors something or other. If you were "dumb" or

parentless or misunderstood, you might find yourself in remedial something. And that's the pack you ran with all day.

Parents of junior highers didn't come to school much,
maybe because they couldn't negotiate a relationship with anyone on campus, full to overflowing with half-crazed inmates.
In many junior highs, PTOs and PTAs cease to exist, and fewer
parents come to open house. Maybe, discomfited, they remember their owns pains and idiocies those umpteen years ago when
they were in the same junior high boat.

Traditional junior highs do not work anymore, if they ever
did, and moving ninth graders to high schools in order to make
room for sixth graders to join the rat race isn't the answer. Instead, I pine for some elementary school practices: self-contained classrooms, longer blocks of uninterrupted time, more
hands-on learning, more integrated subjects, fewer students for
a few teachers to teach all day long, everyone getting to know
and feel responsible for one another.

Those big schools were built under the faulty assumption
that bigger is cheaper. One principal, one utility bill, one cafeteria crew. But the debits outweigh the credits. The more kids
in one place, the more disciplinarians. More principals, cops,
counselors, special services personnel are hired to manage the
crowds. Volunteers, like foster grandparents, found in every
elementary school, are scarce as hounds' teeth in junior high.
They're probably intimidated by the numbers packed in school
like tuna in Star-Kist cans.

Once, a group of teachers from Japan came to Cheyenne
and wanted to tour a typical American junior high. My principal, bless him, came to my room — it was my prep period —
and asked me to show them around. I dreaded the job. It was
Friday afternoon, last period. It was spring, so juices were flowing inside and out. To top it all off, it was Crazy Day, meaning

students could dress up in some wild costume depicting '50s attire. In short, the kids were wound up.

I met my guests at the front door, all of us smiling and bowing at one another. Off we went down the long math hall. I figured that'd be a safe place to find some real work going on. Wrong! In the first room, two boys were standing in the front of the room, squared off, wearing boxing gloves. The teacher looked up at us with glazed eyes.

Oops! Bad day here. I led my gaggle off to the next room. Kids were sitting atop desks, on the radiator, talking away the last ten minutes of the week. In another room kids were watching a movie, in another they were arguing about the best make of cars.

The bell was about to ring letting school out. I needed to find a safe place for my entourage out of harm's way when the floodgates of hell were raised, so I herded them into a little alcove out of the hallway. Some kids dashed out of rooms a few minutes early, clanging the doors against the walls. When the bell rang, the kids hit the halls in earnest, running off their adrenaline-powered joy. Seeing our school from the visitors' eyes, I began to wonder in earnest about how, and why, we do things the way we do.

DOUG CAUGHT IN TIME WARP

Doug, like Steve, was another small boy, but he coped by ignoring all of us completely. When he came to, which he rarely did, he acted surprised to find himself in junior high school. He wasn't done playing and imagining fantastic journeys far away from the realities of school. I watched Doug work his way down the hallway to the lunchroom. There he was, a boy who hadn't yet shaved, applied deodorant, or tamed down his cowlick. He shuffled along behind a gaggle of ninth grade girls — Laura and her crew — probably giggling about sexual adventures last Friday night. I saw an arm snake out of the mash of bodies and hit him in the back of the head, lurching him forward into the girls.

From my vantage point against the hall, I saw all their vulnerabilities — the girls worrying about red stains on the backs of their white pants, the boys feeling too puny to peel off their shirts in PE, the seventh graders worrying about their locker combinations, everyone sniffing the air, using that special adolescent radar to detect the rise and fall of their social standing.

Doug's defense against the hullabaloo was to check out, mentally. He just wasn't there. He spent so much time fantasizing I was surprised he could find his way home to supper. His writing was never first-person narrative, never about his own real-life experiences. Instead, he wrote wild tales about superheroes, crosses between flora and fauna, with some human traits thrown in. He never paid attention and he never combed his hair. That's how disconnected he was from the classroom and his social condition. Doug created a hiatus, a place in his head to be for a while until something shook him awake — puberty or future responsibilities.

I gave Doug his poem gift.

Doug's
off on vacation at his desk sometimes.
He wants to write his own way
no limits
and his story of the gruesome, man-eating tree
proves he should.
He learned to be in la-la land at school.

Elementary school
forced him to color in the lines of very narrow hallways.
Junior high
combed his hair flat, taming boyhood cowlicks.
Somehow, in this Halloween House of Horrors,
he manages to have fun.
That alone makes you a Huck Finn grinning hero.

DONIE FEARS SCHOOL

At the beginning of seventh grade, Donie was absent almost every day. The change from her neighborhood elementary to the big junior high did her in. She was scared of forgetting her locker combination. She was scared of the giant ninth graders lording over the hallways. She was scared of forgetting what homework was assigned in what class. Fear made her sick.

One day, with Donie present, I told the class about an experiment I remembered from some psychology text, about how these experimenters wanted to test the stress levels of parents who came to junior high open house. They hooked their parent-subjects up to skin-sensitive equipment and had them do some visual imagery about their own junior high days. The needles on those instruments just had a jumping fit. Fears, real or imagined, loom around the corners in secondary schools, and grownups still remember.

Eventually Donie started coming to school and staying. She wrote fiendishly in her journal, all about growing up out in the country. Her insight was remarkably perceptive for a thirteen-year-old. She told about how her mother fashioned a switch and faked like she would use it just to get Donie on the school bus in first grade. Donie was afraid of the bus driver who had a funny nose. She told about how she got sick every single time they went on a trip to see her grandma — even her stomach was sensitive to change.

I, too, grew up in the country and, like Donie, was the designated garbage burner. One time after school, we talked about our common experiences. We'd been working on the school newspaper, and Donie was waiting for a ride. "Were you ever afraid to take out the garbage at night?" She nodded her head. "Night sure comes early in the winter." I showed her a little poem I'd written about my terrors.

Going out toward the deep darkness
with the trash
I'm confidence, the light house at my back, whistling
to still the small fear.
I dump and turn
my back vulnerable against the listening night.
I pick up speed racing no breath for whistling,
to the pool of back porch light and screened safety
in the nick of time
slam the door on the fingers of fear.
Taking a deep breath,
I whistle into the house
hiding my wheezing weakness.

Thus began our poem conversations. Back and forth. I wrote one; Donie wrote one.

Did you ever wonder that stars
maybe feel our eyes pull up?
Did you ever wonder that moons
know they pull our blood like tides?

Did you ever wonder that green grass knows
it pulls us flat to the earth?
Sometimes I think
stars, moons, grass
know more than me.

I wrote to her during our poem exchange before Christmas break. The unsaid message in this poem is how much I admire Donie's ability to bounce back and right herself.

113

Donie
a gentle girl, rare in junior high schools
so busy manufacturing cookie-cutter kids.
It made you sick at first.
Your mom wrote excuses for you.
Days at a time you stayed home in bed
during your seventh grade year of adjustment.
The miracle?
You came back and landed a spot on the honor roll.
You survived school
without hardening your heart.

Today, Donie is a wonderful and wise kindergarten teacher, gently ushering the little ones into the world of school.

SHANE, THE GRADE GRUNGER

"What was the poem you read, about the wheelbarrow?" Shane was busy at the computer, word processing.

"What poem? Are you sure I read it?"

"Yeah, it had to be you. You're the only one who reads poems to me."

Shane killed himself for a 4.0 grade average. His mother called me a few weeks after school started to be sure I knew the kind of stress Shane put on himself. I told her I knew he coveted A's, but, according to the Stanford Diagnostic Reading Test, Shane's reading ability was average; according to the district writing test, his writing was average. No matter, this kid would not settle for average grades.

I wrote this poem for Shane. Then I decided not to give it to him. No sense in giving him more of my opinion than he could tolerate.

Shane, your mom
called alerting
me to your quest for straight A's.
I said I know
but hinted, so as not to make her mad, that
self respect and deep learning
shouldn't be sacrificed to the GPA god.
Said: What a tricky balance helping a boy know
quantity isn't quality.
We all use fake mile markers
on the muddy road of life,
like:
What car do you drive? Are those Guess jeans?
It's almost un-American of me to think
that coveting after A's is
a dead end in this school puzzle.
You know those Pizza Hut mazes kids draw on with a
*   pencil line?*
Sometimes you bump smack into a dead end.
Grades alone won't take you everywhere you want to be.

Because he loved right answers so much, Shane was po-
etry-phobic, worrying that I might give him a B for a reason he
couldn't even fathom. He was much more comfortable with
true/false tests, one clear right answer to memorize. But he relaxed once he realized he wouldn't be tested nor asked to analyze. "Just listen." That's all I asked of him. Poetry offered Shane
the idea that he could play with language. He quit tying himself into knots, trying to be perfect the first time around. I got
a kick out of watching him squint his eyes and move his words
around here and there, like furniture, just to see the effect.

Something about reading poetry enriches the air in the
classroom. The words in the poems, the shape of them, crop
up in student writing.

The day at the computer he was composing an imitation
of William Carlos Williams' "Red Wheelbarrow."

Wheelbarrow:
So much depends
upon
a red wheel
barrow
glazed with rain
water

beside the white
chickens

Shane's version was fresh as peppermint:

So much depends
upon the white lifesaver

glazed with sugar coating.
I taste winter.

Shane fell in love that ninth-grade year, with Melissa, a pretty, peppy cheerleader, and he was just as intense about her as he was about grades. He wrote this poem, published it in the classroom anthology:

Long long ago
three months
my life shot up like a rocket
for
when I asked
you said yes.

Melissa loved Shane — for a month or so. Then, in typical ninth-grade style, she broke up with him two days after he wrote his poem.

Shane was devastated, for a few hours. But he was spunky and he'd learned, partly through poetry writing, to go a little easier on himself. The writing helped him figure out what he was thinking — and *how* he thought. Maybe more than any other kind of writing, the poetry allowed him to be free enough to feel the power of words, a liberation that perked up his other writing. He was learning to balance straight-line thinking with playfulness and imagination.

Writing was such an important learning tool for my junior high students. It helped them keep their footing. They needed to write every day just to keep up with themselves, to move all their learning into consciousness. Junior high minds, like Shane's, are in a waking-up stage. They still remember the times tables and the names of states and capitals memorized in elementary school, but their minds are at a different place. The "Ah-ha!" learning happens more and more often. When those book and school concepts connect with the students' inarticulated knowing, their faces look like they just awoke from hibernation.

Shane kept getting A's in my class, but his jaw relaxed and he quit hanging out at my desk arguing over every lost half point.

MIGHTY MORPHIN TRAVELERS

Teaching in junior high taught me about emotional roller coaster rides. Even though kids looked like they were morphing at the speed of light, catapulting around blind corners, their core selves were somewhere inside, intact. Once I talked with Brian, my student teacher, about how sometimes I had this feeling. Maybe if I looked closely at Shane, or Donie or Doug, squinting my eyes in concentration, I could project them safely into some future place with all their unique inner flavors intact.

After we talked, I wrote a poem and shared it with Brian.

Beam Me Up, Teach,
I love them,
these blatant busybodies,
awkward child-men of our species.
Their split hooves tap a constant rhythm
down the corridors of youth.
Riding the rapids, they abandon safety for experience.
What scars? They shrug.

They charge every red sea,
expecting water walls to part.
I'm an inanimate object to them,
a life preserver,
ready to buoy their heads above the water
before they submerge on the third count.

Originally, Brian had wanted to teach high school, but he's teaching junior high instead, out in California. I picture him on his roller coaster ride, holding on for dear life. Maybe even throwing food at a faculty party.

CHAPTER SEVEN

The Assembly Line

I LOVE junior high kids, their eccentricities bright as halogen lamps. They're still young enough to be pretty transparent; by high school they become walking onions, layer after layer protecting their tender centers.

Enter my present classroom.

Over there sits Bud. He's a skinhead with hair who subscribes to some pretty strange reading material. He spouts these "facts" about white superiority, his piercing blue eyes mocking the other kids' bleeding heart concerns, as he calls them, about prejudice, ecology, animal rights. He's been kicked out of his house, works all night at the Little America truck stop to support himself. I loan him my old computer so, after he closes at night, he can write and hopefully pass my class before the assembly line moves him to the refuse pile.

A few rows away in the same class is Paula. She works at Little America, too. In spite of the fact that they are coworkers,

Bud points some of his razor-sharp comments her way. Paula's mother, on welfare 14 of the last 17 years, is white; her father is black. He left ten years ago. Paula is the editor of our school newspaper. I write her letters of recommendation. Already she has college scholarships — a dream beyond the reach of her mother and sisters who did not graduate from high school.

I try to create a classroom where Bud and Paula can meet eye to eye and learn.

It's not easy. They both come to class with a truckload of baggage, but that's not the only problem. A big part of the reason it's so hard to teach Bud is because of the system. Fashioned on the concept of Henry Ford's assembly lines, many American secondary schools are like factories, complete with bells. The principals are the foremen. The different subjects — math one period, English the next — are the isolated tasks we linemen perform with mind-numbing routine. Sometimes I get the feeling that the system regards Paula and Bud as refrigerators. The Paula Product, despite production difficulties, works great. The Bud Brand must be recalled.

The isolation of the factory school is hard on students like Paula and Bud, and it's hard on teachers. Two years after I began teaching in the local high school, I met Brenda. I was dimly aware of her presence in the building, but I didn't know her. No way to, stuck as I was, way down a long English hall, miles away from her long social studies hall. Here it was March and we finally connected.

Her story spilled all over me. A transplant from a local elementary school, she hated the coldness of high school. Everything seemed wrong: She had 150 kids in five classes, a whole new batch each semester. She traveled — no room of her own, no desk of her own, always an intruder in someone else's territory. Just taking roll every period took valuable time, and before she finished, kids started eyeing the clock, wishing the 50 minutes away. "How can I get to know the kids? How can I teach them until I get to know them?" she asked the principal.

Get to know the kids? The principal's eyes were blank. The question seemed irrelevant on the assembly line.

American high schools are predicated on the notion that students are objects moving through a production line. Over here we attach a fender, we call it science. Over there, headlights, we call it social studies. When the student come out the other end, they have all their parts. Their transcripts prove it, listing each credit, neat as a warehouse inventory sheet.

121

Contrast Brenda's story with Joanie's. My friend Joanie teaches all-day kindergarten. Talk about a different world! A few years ago she had a little girl in her room, Latitia, a victim of sexual abuse. Every day when school let out, Joanie walked outside with Latty, held her hand to the very edge of the playground. Then, they waved and waved at each other until Latty's red coat disappeared down the street. One afternoon as Joanie waved, Latty turned around. Her little legs pumped like pistons as she ran back into Judy's arms. "God blesses you, Mrs. Thom," Latty whispered into the warmth of Joanie's neck. "God blesses you."

The elementary schools, though they too are institutionalized and run the risk of dehumanizing people, nevertheless afford more human interaction, more integrated learning, more connection between the learner and the world. That's partly because the school is smaller, partly because Brenda is with Latitia all day, and partly because elementary schools make no apologies about being student-centered.

Back in the 1950s, I attended a high school fashioned after a factory, too, only mine housed about 350 kids instead of almost two thousand. In those days we responded more amiably to being herded around. For one thing, over half of us were farm kids, and school seemed blissfully restful compared to the chores that waited for us at home. Also, maybe our nightmares of Nagasaki, Mathausen, and Korea, along with our dad's military uniforms hanging in the recesses of our cedar closets at home, kept us in line. Even so, separate notebooks for separate classes and bells ringing us to and fro was starting to grow old by the time I graduated in 1962. Here we are at the turn of the century, and the same old school system creaks along, even though the Industrial Revolution is over. Modern factories are changing, retooling their assembly lines into teams, creating environments that foster engagement and commitment. Schools still creak along oblivious, for the most part, to these changes.

My teaching colleague, Brenda, was right. What we both wanted was a system that would help us really reach and teach Bud and Paula, just like Brenda reached Latty.

Like fish in an aquarium, we're limited by our glass world, and the water grows pretty toxic.

BLACK BUD

For three days after the April 18, 1995 bombing in Oklahoma City, Bud was absent from English. After he returned, he said that he went down to view the bomb site. I couldn't shake the feeling that, in his mind, Bud blew up the Oklahoma federal building.

Like a Rottweiler whose jaws lock around a victim's arm, Bud's mind clenched down on certain ideas, held them inviolate. He had sclerosis of the mind. The outer crust around his ideas was so impenetrable that I feared he'd blow a fuse, maybe blow up some other people, too. At graduation, Bud didn't walk down the aisle. I felt disloyal to him, but I caught myself scanning the top-row seats in the gym looking for a familiar black hat and a long shiny object of death aimed at someone on the stage or in the crowd.

Bud hated school — sneered when he said the word. He hadn't hated elementary school. His troubles started in junior high when his wizardry led him into deep trouble. He hacked his way into some classified computer information and was banned from the lab forever. Exiled. Furthermore, Bud wasn't a kid who took naturally to making mental connections, integrating learning into some kind of meaningful pattern. In Bud's head, everything stayed neatly packaged and divorced from everything else, and the segregated subjects of junior high and high school exacerbated his single-minded literalness. What a brain this kid had, and what a lot of it he wasted! He needed a poem. I gave him this one. I thought he might crumple it up and shove it deep in the pocket of his black trench coat. But he didn't. He seemed pleased, in a grim way.

123

> Bud
> All in black
> from head to toe.
> I've never seen you without your black hat hiding your
>   eyes.
> After the federal building blew up in Oklahoma City
> you were absent.
> I worried about you in my dreams.
> Later you said you went down there just to see,
> just to see.
> In junior high they kicked you permanently out of the
>   computer lab,
> you, a virus infecting the whole school—
> screwed up grades
> scrambled attendance.

Last year the police came to your house
something about hacking your way into some private
　　　system.
"African Americans" is a curse on your lips.
The way you say it smears excrement in the room.
Paula looks at you, unblinking.
"African Americans bring down this country."
You bury us in statistics: crime, welfare, abuse, teenage
　　　pregnancy, sexually transmitted disease.
All a "black problem," in your view.
You live somewhere on Internet
connected through waves and wires,
hate pungent as burning human hair,
thoughts encased in bullets.
I sit face to face and ask,
"Bud, what about next year?"
"I'll enlist in the Marines," you say, eyes jerking away
　　　from my close contact
before you drop down the mask.
"Well, don't settle for cheap answers," I say.
I'll be
wondering
wondering
for years.
Where are you, Bud?
Were you able to move off the ledge
with such narrow footing?

My poem was a prayer for Bud. I hoped he could read how much I wanted him to find his way out of the dark. Bud, break that eggshell around your dead-end ideas. Outside is a bigger, wider world view.

Fortunately, Bud's story didn't end with high school graduation. This Christmas, three years after he graduated, I got a long letter from him. Though the words didn't come right out and say so, the message between the lines was clear: I'm OK, Mrs. Lain. I'm going to church again. I'm doing fine, don't worry any more about me. He even included pictures of himself walking along a Florida beach. That's where he was stationed after boot camp.

JENNIFER TRIMS HER SAILS

Unlike Bud, most students consciously admit they want school to be much more than fragmented learning. They're desperate to piece their lives together. They want to quilt a pattern that makes sense. Take Jennifer the artist.

Over and over in her journal, Jennifer wrote, "I feel like I don't belong in this time." Or, "I'm out of sync here. This just isn't me." In high school she felt like she was being buried alive in a coffin. Her only breathing space was in art, and English, if we got to write poems. Oh, the talent in those stubby fingers. She created ceramic sculptures, pregnant-looking pods swaying as if they were under water. She lived in that studio, before school, during lunch, after school.

Her body wasn't quite right — flat-chested and dainty on top, big-boned from the waist down. She got picked on by the girls in junior high and finally decided to really give them something to gawk at. She shaved her head bald.

I hoped this poem might comfort her, maybe validate her feelings, open up future's door.

Jennifer
You feel
all the pulling pulling people

hands grabbing
to strip your clothes
claws scratching skin
invading inner space.
Eyes judge every angle
analyze laundry lists
of definitions
with eyes and tongues
pointing
adding subtracting.
In school
all is posturing
count the beats, don't feel 'em
a parody of passion.
You say no genius could survive,
not Beethoven
Van Gogh
Shakespeare
Einstein.
You run outside —
Leap into another time.

Three times Jennifer tried to get "exterminated" from school. She finally succeeded the day she piled her books and papers in the middle of the hall and set fire to them. Afterward, she continued her art in her teacher's home studio. A few months after her expulsion, I ran into Jennifer working at the Dairy Queen. She wanted me to know that she'd had some poetry published. "I'm going to Community School, Mrs. Lain … thought you'd get a kick out of knowing." Community School, a one-room, nontraditional school with fifty students, was an alternative to traditional high school.

That was two years ago. This year during Christmas break, we unwittingly bumped elbows at Wal-Mart. After our reunion scene, she told me she was in college studying computer science. She made the leap, she told me, from right-braininess to left. "Art and poetry, they'll always be my heart, Mrs. Lain, but I gotta get a job now. I'm gonna be normal. Me, normal? That's an oxymoron, huh?" She grinned at herself, at the irony of it all. I'm so glad that the art and poetry sustained Jennifer during her years of stumbling blind.

Ben-and-Joe Teach Me Yin-Yang

Ben and Joe checked into class late. They hesitated at the door of twelfth-grade composition three days after the semester started. They'd taken a detour via British Literature. The teacher said they weren't capable of handling his class. They just didn't fit the profile. Kicked them out.

Something about the factory school fosters incivility, even among the teachers. Probably it's the size, the impersonal nature inherent when kids dash from room to room all day long.

Ben and Joe had met years before in the resource room at Frontier Park Elementary. Fast friends, they limped along together through one school building after another, holding each other up. Even though the guidance counselor said they really didn't "belong" in my college-bound composition class either, they stayed, and I counted myself lucky to know these warmhearted boys. They taught me how to teach them.

Their essays were murky morasses. I needed hip-high waders to slog through their essay writing, and no matter how hard we worked, they didn't improve much. So I tried something different — they did their research, and then, instead of writing in the expository mode, they wrote stories on their topics.

For some reason, their brains were hard-wired to understand how to write a story. The shape of their ideas just came out in what they wrote without their conscious application of structure. The writing must have done them good; later on, when we tackled essays again, the organization of their writing started shaping up. The mechanics, usage, and spelling still lagged behind. To write, these boys would need to be handcuffed to a spell check.

They taught me more than how to teach them; they taught me about life. Ben and Joe were deep into fantasy novels, especially the *Dragonlance Chronicles*. They shared their books with me, and though I'm not crazy about fantasy, I learned why they loved the books: the themes dealt with the struggle of good and evil, and, since these boys were throwbacks to the days of the knights in shining armor, the fantasy world made complete sense to them. We talked after class almost every day. Once I said, "I think all your novels are about good winning against evil."

Gently, Ben corrected me. "Excuse me, Mrs. Lain, but it's not about winning or losing. It's about balance, that's all. It's about balance."

Ah, yes. Yin and yang. The darkness makes the light possible, and vice versa. I think I got it.

My poem for Ben and Joe celebrated their warmth.

So much depends upon Ben's and Joe's arrival in my
    room.
In my daily rush
they
(Have you read Dragonlance Chronicles?*)*
Will we write stories in here?)
ground me.

Ben and Joe remind me of my pet Nicki's
*   brown-eyed adoration —*
evil and good balanced.
Boys, I agree:
Sometimes, I'd rather live in Dragonlance worlds than
*   here.*

Ben and Joe hungered to connect with big ideas. Struggling with the system that labeled them and placed them in skills-only classes, they wanted to get beyond all that hammering on details they couldn't do very well anyway — spell, read fast, write neatly. They wanted to inquire and ponder and connect with the whole panorama of human experience, shaped by huge currents of thought and manifested in art, music, literature. This they wanted more than some of my grade grungers, on their way to military academies.

JASON THE WILTED GARDENIA

The year I taught Jason was a rough one for our high school. Some of my fellow teachers were chasing down the principal who was running for his life to preserve his job. The pack closed in for the kill. Whispered meetings in hallways. "Climate" surveys in our mailboxes. The superintendent was called in. Just as I did as a kid at the movies when the cowboys were about to kill the Indians, I shut my eyes and braced myself to avoid seeing the bloodshed.

Jason, a transfer from Hawaii, rode the bus to school, which meant he arrived way early. With no home away from home, he feigned sleep, like a vagrant, in the hallway near my room until I arrived to unlock the door and let him in. Advantage: he was never tardy. Disadvantage: he overheard the teachers gossip. Sitting there in the hallway, propped up by the wall, eyes closed, head bent to his knees, he overheard worrisome words. One day he alluded to what he'd heard in the hall, asking me, "Mrs. Lain, are you a maverick? Or, do you go with the flow around here?" I looked up at him, blinking a little to clear my head, trying to figure out what he was getting at.

Though his forte was not the persuasive essay, he was an amazing poet. During one poetry writing interlude, sandwiched amidst the required essays, he wrote an extended metaphor — one that referenced the hall talk he'd overheard — and his writing knocked my socks off. My snippets to students were a teaching tool; his writing had the potential to be art. His poem is proof of his perceptiveness and his skill.

> Hunger drives them
> twisting their stomachs
> hollow pain
> she lion shoots like liquid gold fire
> in the startled face of quiet grazing
> ripping tendons
> snapping bones
> snarling in greedy need

Jason and I became poem pen pals. We wrote back and forth to one another because both of us believed that communication is a two-way process. I wrote a poem for Jason, commiserating with him a little about the frigid temperatures.

> Jason
> You sit in the hall like a withered gardenia
> every day

waiting for school to start.
You moved here this semester from Maui.
Winter this year is unusually white
sharp-toothed.
The wind redmarks your brown skin.
You bow your head
look asleep
overhear hallway gossip.
Teachers standing hall attention
shrink everyone
to goose bumps.
Walking by, you feel the chill
of judgment.
You shiver.
The school is winter inside.
You warm your hands at my desk
every day after class
as long as possible
before braving the cold hall,
no winter jacket yet.

Since his dad was in the military, the family's Wyoming tenure was short-lived. By year's end, off they moved to Florida. I hope there the air felt more like home.

DAVID, THE WORK DODGER

I watched David. From the first day he acted like he was waiting. I was new at Western High. I didn't understand the system, but David did. He listened to the old-timers, upper classmen, out in the hall. There *was* a way out of the work in sophomore English, in spite of what the registration book said: "To graduate from Western High, every student must pass Introduction to Writing, a sophomore course."

Though the "rule" sounded official, it turned out there were several ways to avoid this writing class, and David knew if he sat and vegetated long enough, did absolutely nothing, had his mom call, say, in October right after the first grade report, pretty soon the cavalry would charge in, and he'd be saved. Off he'd be whisked to a scaled-down English, maybe the computer-programmed course with electronic worksheets and precious little reading and writing, talking and thinking. He'd be off somewhere doing something easier, fulfilling his own prophecy that he was a dumbhead.

The counselor said the reading course was vital to keep kids like David from dropping out of school, but David dropped out anyway.

When I went to his new classroom to return his writing portfolio, I was stunned. The room was full of boys, and almost all of them were kids of color, like David. Maybe the school meant well, but David's label seemed to give him more license to act out and then drop out.

The classroom was lined with computers, and those can be powerful tools to write and find research, but the screen showed exercises practicing capitalization. Not a single book was in sight, no creative writing on display, no student writing journals on the shelf. It didn't make sense to me to put David, who didn't read fluently, in a room with other boys who didn't like to read either. Instead of reading and writing for fun, for sharing, for gaining and transmitting information, David and his cohorts filled in blanks, practiced "basic skills." I wanted David back in fourth period. He had stories to write. He had opinions about life. But he didn't come back.

At the end of the year, though David didn't stay in school that long, he would have taken a post-test, another "bubble-in-the-right-answer" test on, say, contractions. David might have shown growth on that test, especially after practicing the apostrophe all year. But I would bet my life that spelling *you're* and *your* correctly on electronic worksheets wouldn't translate to David's writing. He could circle the correct *you're* or *your* till the cows came home. Then he'd turn right around and misspell *you're* in his first draft. There he'd sit, hunched over his paper, chewing on his lip. At this stage of his writing, he was concentrating on how to make the words resemble his ideas. He'd be lucky to remember to put capitals at the beginnings of sentences, let alone where to put the apostrophes, at least on his first drafts.

133

We school people struggle with systems like remedial courses and tracking that are not supported by research or common sense. These programs tend to take on a life of their own — and a constituency. Tough to change them, let alone dismantle the operations, no matter how good or bad they are for David. Systems don't want to change.

I got caught in a tug of war over David, and lost.

Giselle, the counselor, pulled on one of David's arms, and I pulled on the other. She won. He got what he wanted in the short run, a fast track through the year. After he left, I was mad and sad. You can tell by this poem — one I never gave him.

David
you were the prize in my tug-of-war
with the system.
I lost.
She wanted your body in her program.
You wanted an easy slide to graduation.

Unlikely allies in this conspiracy of failure.
You can do the work I offer
but won't.
In the hallway you've heard The Truth.
Sit tight. Daydream, if you want.
Eventually the rescue squad will come
and dump you in a place
where catatonic fog earns you at least a C.
They'll fuel that class with your lazy-ass self
and justify its existence.
If we dumby-down your curriculum enough, you'll stay
*   in school,*
and we can have the money your head counts.
That's the theory.
The theory doesn't pan out.
"Once a quitter always a quitter,"
someone once said.
You believe it.

David escaped, and I turned back to the waiting class. Somehow his empty desk felt like an indictment. "Well, you have to expect casualties," someone said. My question: Why do the losses have to come from the ranks of innocent kids?

RAY, THE QUANTUM PHYSICIST

Ray was an avid outdoorsman, and he thought like a scientist. Wyoming was his science lab, all 97,000 square miles of it. What he learned from the natural world is that everything is connected. "Hey, Mrs. Lain, did you know that everything sort of absorbs a little of everything else? Our atoms are thin-skinned. Our skin is permeable, too." Ray tucked me under his wing to tutor me on the fine points of quantum physics.

I'm no scientist, but I've always wondered why ideas seem to be in the air. A writer friend told me she wrote a short story about this alien that came to earth, assumed an earthling's body, and fell in love before he was beamed back to his spaceship. A few weeks later, she went to the movies, and, lo and behold, there was Jeff Bridges in *The Star Man*.

Ray explained his rationale to me. "Well, it makes sense. Since everything is connected, ideas might be like energy moving through the air."

135

Maybe Ray is right about invisible connections. Sometimes when we are all engrossed in reading or writing, so quiet I can almost hear the dust moving in the sun shafts, I feel like we are all one body, like we are breathing in each other.

Ray assured me I wasn't hallucinating. "Nature has lots of unexplainables. Like, did you know that plants actually scream? Say your geraniums' got bugs." He pointed to the potted plants on the window ledge. "They'd scream. Maybe we can hear them … somehow."

Once, Ray even decided to teach me about fractals. He brought in a piece of graph paper. He'd drawn an identical line in each little box. The overall pattern on the page was the same as the pattern in each little box. Not being a scientist, I mostly understood this fractal concept when Wahling, the art teacher, showed me what she'd done with her impressionistic nature-scape. She took her big painting, cut it up into little round circles, and made decorative pins out of them. The big painting told a story, conveyed a feeling, and so did each little painting. "Wabi Sabi. That's what it is," she said. "As above, so below."

Though Ray was brilliant, he worried about flunking biology, a class where he outlined chapters and filled in study guides. He was a fish out of water at school, restlessly staring out the window, never scoring well on multiple choice tests.

Ray,
you can't stand too much of school
Learning that straight-line way is not for you.
That's why you wade into the Wind River.
Rushing energy flows
around your thighs,
pushes you enough
to keep you on your toes,
teaches your body about balance.
You look into the river
rocks grooming themselves smooth against one another,
water resting for a moment against a damp bank,
grass fingers reaching up to the truth of the sun.
You crane your neck, looking upward,
blue sky, red walls
all around in a sweep.
You know and feel it all at once —
your science lesson.

In the poem I tried to hold a mirror up to Ray's eyes to explain how much he knew about the natural world — the dynamics of balance in the ecosystem; the interrelationship of water and rock, grass and sun; the energy of parts reacting with the whole. He was a natural-born scientist, but he accepted the school's version of his achievement — the D in assembly-line biology. He just didn't fully appreciate all he knew.

HAL DROPPED OUT

Hal became a digit in the district's dropout statistics. The number grows in spite of our attempts to staunch the flow, like creating more alternatives to earn a diploma. I learned about his childhood on a sugar-beet farm; he loved his life in the country so much that he wrote about it in his journal. His nostalgia was especially poignant because his folks sold the farm and moved to the tiny town of Pavilion to open an auto shop.

After a semester of twelfth grade, he quit. He got tired of reducing his life to counting time. Couldn't stand all the barbed-wire restraints: a certain number of credits to graduate, a certain amount of seat time to count him as a student, a certain total of points marching across a teacher's grade book. I wrote to Hal to try to talk about real learning.

Hal
You count like a miser counts his money
the steps to graduation
the hours and credits
as if the total could equal
the sun traveling the sky.
You can't count the parts of love
Such arithmetic subtracts.
I have something for you,
here cupped in my hands:
Yellow flight against blue sky
I must let it go.
Hurry!
I am only waiting for a moment for you to come here
*   and see.*

Hall still quit school, but today he's one of the best mechanics in the county. I saw him at the class reunion. He told me he still had that poem I wrote him. Said he figured it out finally. "School was just so many moves on the Monopoly board. I got tired of banking credits. But last year I took a personal writing class at the community college. It reminded me of you, how you got so excited about learning. Got me goin'. Now, I'm gonna write a book!"

AKIKO, A METAPHOR OF JAPAN

Some of my foreign students are secretly taken aback at the lenience, the diversity, of American schools. Interpreting every joke as an insult to the teacher, they don't know whether to laugh, so they smile behind their hands, at least for a while. They test the waters a little, never knowing quite where the edges of appropriate behavior lie. If you asked Japanese Akiko to define America, she'd have a one-word answer — chaos.

An exchange student from Japan, Akiko came to live with our family. I nudged her, encouraged her stories and absorbed them like my thirsty lawn drinks water. Our lives were so different. In our home, Gayle, my husband, does not always occupy the seat at the head of the table. In hers the father is always number one. In ours the brothers are not always the second in command in the father's absence, receiving the second best morsels of food. In hers, whenever the father is not around, the brother's word is law. We blew Akiko's mind.

School blew her mind, too. The American kids' lack of discipline floored her. She told her classmates about the sixth grade teacher who for some reason didn't like Akiko, this shy, withdrawn girl, and slapped her so hard across the left side of her face that he broke her eardrum.

"Did you sue?" My American kids were incredulous when she shook her head. "No," she said. That would never be done. Anyway, she got off lucky. The teacher threw a desk at another kid, broke his jaw.

"No one pressed charges? The teacher wasn't fired?" The kids were in shock. I'll bet secretly they thought those Japanese kids were wimps for putting up with such abuse.

Akiko's hair had a hint of a wave. Because her hair wasn't pure Japanese, she'd suffered terribly. She said old ladies on the commuter train clucked and shook their heads in disapproval. Maybe Akiko was not a pure blood. Maybe she — horrors — waves her hair on purpose. This was not to be done until girls were in college, if then.

But for all the rigid conformity in looks and behavior, there was an upside to life in Japan. Akiko told about once when her sister lost her purse in Tokyo. It was mailed home intact, all the money inside to the last coin. No reward or thank you was expected. And Akiko's lips crimped into a little smile when she said, "I could go lie down on the streets of Tokyo, at three in the morning, and no one would bother me." That's how safe Tokyo is!

When we went shopping in Denver, she nervously scanned the tops of buildings, flinching at each loud sound. She fully expected a sniper to appear any second and blow us away. This America, Akiko believed, is full of out-of-control people.

I wrote about Akiko in my journal a few days after she returned to Japan. Reflecting on the poem, I see that somehow by listening with inner ears, I learned more about Japan from Akiko than I ever did in all the history books. So did the students. Now, we can't watch dispassionately the news about Japan, for when we hear the word Japan, we see the face of our friend.

Akiko
you came inside,
girl of Japan.
I studied you —
extrapolating from every downward look, your hands'
*   habits*
a metaphor of Japan.
Finally I knew
the haiku
the Kamikaze mind
the severe pruning of the bonsai.
When you left
we both cried
but you held your tears inside.

Once in a great while, I suffer acute nostalgia for a foreign place like Japan where people stay in line, or a past time in America, such as the '50s, when picket fences marked the edges of propriety and boys wore their shirts tucked in. But if we revert to a time of too much uniformity now, the good old days would feel pretty claustrophobic. Maybe a factory school would work if we were all just exactly alike. Maybe. But that's not going to happen, and we don't even want it to. So much uniformity would be unbearable. Sometime soon, maybe the factory schools of Japan and America will evolve into some kind of learning communities where we can honor differences.

FRACTAL LESSON

Despite my hair-pulling frustrations with secondary schools, how they make teaching and learning so complicated,

I love teaching. I'm glad I got to know Ray and the rest of them. How varied they are. How fun and poignant their stories. No matter how persistently the system tries to depersonalize us, the best teaching, especially of language, is an intimate experience. Through the writing, lines of words spinning out like spider webs from No. 2 pencils, I read the student's brain. As I listen, I read the words and the reasoning behind the words. This intent listening is love. As we learn language from infancy on, love shelters us and propels us forward.

The assembly-line school makes teaching difficult, but not impossible. When I get it right, the single cell of my room, afloat in the whole school organism, is lit with a kind of yellow glow. The reading, writing, and sharing connect us to one another and to a world we are learning to inherit.

141

CHAPTER EIGHT

Stars

I N 1959 my mother paid for my singing lessons. That was the year we left the farm. Overnight I became a town girl, and this new form didn't fit. I felt suffocated in town. Instead of 360 acres of alfalfa, we had a lawn measured in square feet. In town I couldn't outdistance my house-penned turbulence, jumping irrigation ditches, leaping over sagebrush in a mad dash to keep pace with the wind. Town life was flat. Flat, black asphalt streets. Bland tract houses, alike except for varying shades of pastel paint. Inside, look-alike Betty Crocker wives performed similar rituals of cooking, cleaning, and playing bridge, all permed, all wearing little aprons.

My mother was relieved — no more milk separators to wash, no more manure on the linoleum floor to mop up, no more cows to chase home at three in the morning. But I was claustrophobic. Mom noticed and decided to find a music teacher for me. Maybe art would fill my void, contain my passion.

Until I could drive the car myself, she dropped me off every Saturday morning at the curb near Mrs. Demerski's little square house. The sidewalk, straight as the part in my hair, split the yellow winter lawn. Mr. Demerski cut that lawn in the fall, straight as a kid's flat-top. A transplant like me, Mrs. Demerski sang at the Met in New York City, a world away, until one day she up and married. Her husband was a furniture salesman and they made their way west, stopping for a few years in rural Powell, Wyoming.

On the first day of my lessons, I stepped into her dim living room and stopped still. In the silence I sensed the wild grief and ecstasy of notes shaped into rhythms, the sounds and shapes mirroring life. Those waves of music contrasted sharply with the monotone of small town dinner-table conversation.

Mrs. Demerski herself was large, blonde and regal. She taught me as if my small talent were holy. In the dimmed living room, the piano light casting a round spotlight on the musical score, I moved from scales, to training pieces, to arias. For an hour on Saturday morning, I was Puccini's Mimi or Tosca's Carmen. I'm sure she knew my talent wouldn't take me to the Met. Maybe to a lifetime of singing in community choirs, but not the met. I loved the Saturday morning lessons anyway, and I think she did, too.

She taught me how to sing the high C with my fingertips. "Place the sound here." Singing or speaking, her voice was beautiful. She placed the sensitive pads of my fingertips lightly against her face, in one specific spot — on her cheeks ... under her eyes ... close to her nose ... right over the sinus cavities. There, when she sang the high F, I could feel the sound with my fingers. Then, she placed the fingers lightly to her forehead, right above the eyebrows. She sang the high C.

I felt it! I touched the sound and finally understood how to sing the notes. Fingers against my own forehead, I felt the correct placement and sang the note.

A year after I started taking voice lessons from Mrs. Demerski, she and her husband moved to a small city — a place with a larger stage for her music. But before she left, she taught me with her light touch, how we humans learn through our skin as well as our ears. Lessons from the music teacher taught me to honor human potential in my students, however large or small.

145

LaWanna Sings Down the Stars

Delbert, LaWanna's brother, went to prison for vehicular homicide. I knew him as a wild-eyed boy who sometimes shook his head as if to settle down the buzzing. LaWanna wrote of her grief and shame. She needed some way to clarify what happened to Delbert, to gain some perspective. I wrote to her:

LaWanna
Sitting here in silence
I hear the fabric tearing,
long strips ripping.
I hear the screaming separation.
Today, your brother bangs his head against prison walls.
As a little boy he needed Ritalin
or long moments lying in summer prairie
cradled in the certainty of earth.
But without, "Hush, Dear," calm as a mother's hand,
he raced pell-mell,
careening into a blank wall he mistook for a door.

Like a wind-up toy
he knew his way only
by banging into the legs of authority
immutable as prehistoric stones.
I hear the fabric tear
and yearn for bandages to wrap, hold, heal.

When I wrote to LaWanna, I was thinking of all the boys I knew like Delbert, wondering about the frenzied quivering that seized their brains. LaWanna and I became friendly, which resulted in an invitation to the Second Baptist on Cheyenne's west side to hear her sing. She was radiant in the choir during vespers, her voice soaring over the others, providing winged leadership.

Solo
soprano
voice
pierces the jet-black softness of listening night.
Upon the stage
your feet plant firmly on wooden reality.
Head aloft
you exhale through vibrating chords,
spin sound into space.
That single sound
held aloft on air column
shatters gravity and glass crucibles of time and space
travels through stratosphere of dark awareness.
Beyond the limit of wings
sings your eternal question.
Who am I?

*Your single voice moves yet in the voyage up
on the breath of God.*

My childhood church services were as predictable as Robert's Rules of Order, every word dictated by script, every movement an understatement. LaWanna's church, on the other hand, was a jazz set. One Sunday morning, a beautiful little boy in the pew behind me, his skin like polished walnut, punctuated every "Amen" with a shake of his tambourine. Using no sheet music, the pianist seemed to know in his bones when to join the preacher's voice, lifting his piano chords in a crescendo toward the end of every prayer.

147

Three ladies, their hats backlit by sunshine from the east window, conducted a sort of pre-service service. "Blessed are the poor in spirit for they shall inherit the earth."

"Amen!"

"Whatsoever you do for the least of these my children you do so unto me."

"Amen. Amen."

"We pray for our brothers and sisters, fathers and sons in prison. May they find peace in the blood of the Lamb."

"Oh, Jesus. Amen."

Everything in that service, including LaWanna's solo, was played by ear, by heart.

The preacher told stories proving the power of prayer. He claimed that what goes on in our minds and hearts affects our body and the physical world around us.

All the signs seemed to indicate that prayer did help LaWanna. In her church she was a beam of light, and at school, a place where talk of spirituality was usually met with stiff silence, LaWanna glowed. The church and the school gave her gifts: the church gave her healing prayer and the school gave her formal music training.

She needed both, for things were not good at home. I knew Delbert, had him in class three years before. He was only there six weeks before the principal kicked him out of school. The kid was a forest fire — unpredictable energy shooting sparks in every direction.

LaWanna wrote about him, what it was like around the house with him. He peed through the chain link fence into the neighbor's vegetable garden. Got caught. He was six. He rode his bike off the tin roof of a Quonset hut and broke his leg, a compound fracture. He was nine. He jumped on beds and sofas till they moaned and sagged into lumpy deaths. He was a walking catastrophe. Their dad left when LaWanna was six, Delbert nine. LaWanna's mom, diagnosed with lupus, was often swept into such fatigue that she couldn't think straight, especially when Delbert banged around.

LaWanna found solace in music. She sang. She played the piano. In the steady ticking of the metronome and the musical patterns she could make some sense out of life.

Knowing LaWanna, I learned firsthand about human potential.

DAVID OF GOLIATH CHARMS

David was a natural-born entertainer, and he had great timing. He sang or danced in those two-minute snatches right after we'd close our books and before the bell would ring. Today he's a regular in a Denver dinner theater.

He'd sing at the drop of a hat, and his favorites during those two-minute gigs were his Vacation Bible School songs. As president of the Methodist Youth Fellowship, he knew them all — and loved them: "Zachias was a wee little man, a wee little man was he…." "Climb, climb up Sunshine Mountain, faces all aglow…." "The B. I. B. L. E., yes that's the Book for me…."

He organized a group of girls in the room to play backup. They dubbed themselves David Harlen and the Supremes. They choreographed cool moves, all in two-minute snatches between bells.

David's real quartet performed for Stars of Tomorrow and took first place at both the local and regional levels.

David,
your blue eyes always laugh
even when your face is still.
I walked early this morning
hours before school
alone except for the moon and sun
one entering, one exiting
and thought of you.
How did you learn that everything,
even puberty,
is funny.
You smile even when you whine
about too much homework the night before the Stars
    show.
I'll bet backstage
everyone else shivered
worried about:
What if I've used up all my high Cs, the quota you said
    the Soprano God allowed?
What if teenaged Alzheimer's obliterates all memory of
    song lyrics?

What if the microphone cord becomes an octopus arm
    and trips me up
knocking out front teeth, braces and all?
Your eyes are a laughing sedative.
Your quartet won first place.

Right before the end of the school year, David wrote me a note:

Mrs. Lain,
    When I stand by you I feel you know us better than
we know us. You teach not just about past participles.
David

LONG-LIMBED LISA

Lisa was a ballet dancer. She wanted me to help her with a poem so she could choreograph it to music; then, she presented her research topic to the class through poetry and dance. She'd studied teenage schizophrenia, read *I Never Promised You a Rose Garden* and *Lisa Bright and Dark*. She wrote the following poem, and her presentation, a dance she choreographed to match the words, riveted her classmates.

Lisa
What is it like to be me now?
Well "Melancholy Baby" could've been written
with me in mind.
But a moment ago
I was giggly bubbles
in a cherry Coke
I change a lot now.

What is it like to be me now?
Well, I wouldn't have believed Jesus
if I'd put my whole arm in his side.
But a moment ago
I trusted like a sweet child
holding my daddy's hand.
I change a lot now.
What is it like to be me now?
Well, I'm a sad cynic
feeling more desolate inside a phony grin.
But a moment ago
I thought the world was a hope chest.
I change a lot now.

151

Lisa wrote to me from the University of Utah where she landed a dance scholarship.

Dear Mrs. Lain,
I absorbed a part of you and began to understand the depth and soul within each human being. I took for granted that you'd always be near me to spice up the bland, but I'm gone and I miss you.
Lisa

KELLEY, THE LONG-DISTANCE RUNNER

Kelley was a local track star, a state record breaker. This quiet boy sat in the juices of the class and soaked in all the flavors. Without saying very much, his integrity and discipline permeated the room. He kept everyone honest. During his senior year, his Kansas grandfather died. He spent a lot of time writing about him and his memories of being on the farm. I wrote to him about what he told me, about what seemed to mean most to him:

> *Kelley is a long-distance runner*
> *Some people's lazy lungs beg to sit in front of MTV*
> *Some people's softening biceps benchpress Lay's Potato*
>   *Chips*
> *Some people ride around in noisy cars hollering out*
>   *their windows at each other*
> *Kelley runs*
> *in predawn silence*
> *muscles, lean, clearly defined through thin skin*
> *His feet pound rhythm as steady as a heart beat,*
> *mind turns to Kansas sunrise*
> *long cornfields*
> *Grandfather showing him which ear is ripe*
> *and Grandmother setting out yellow butter, syrup,*
>   *steaming hotcakes*
> *Kelley's discipline is straight as a corn row,*
> *his integrity is steady as Grandma and Grandpa's love.*

I felt pretty sure that at least some of the kids like Kelley learned to value the almost tangible inner self of each person in the classroom.

JULIE'S WORDS

When some students write, beautiful words sprinkle a baptism, like water drops in the air above Yellowstone Falls. Julie was especially talented, for she handled extended word passages with the same expertise.

Julie was a warmhearted poet. Kind of a misplaced hippie, she loved English class, the words, the ideas, the idealism, the personal exploration. Her thoughts were circles and spirals, so she disliked most classes, couldn't fathom linear courses like math and computer science. But she loved English. Julie was built round and full — in an age when wafer-thin was in. I had Julie as a senior, long after the tortured days of junior high when some anonymous hand pinched her big breasts in the packed hallway, during the time her parents up and divorced. During those years from hell, it was her Hispanic grandmother, the one with deep roots, steady faith, and warm tortillas, who kept Julie centered.

153

One day in class a former student, one I'd had two years before, popped in the door to say hello. Impulsively, I kissed her cheek. Most of the kids, writing away in their notebooks, didn't notice, but Julie did, and she wrote this little piece in her journal, marking it with a sticky note so I'd be sure to read it:

Mrs. Lain
motherteacher
kissing a girl on the cheek
like a fawn.
Kiss me, too?
I can be gentle
like whitefluff dandelion too.

At the end of the semester, before the class broke apart for the summer, we all wrote notes to one other, and I jotted a little poem for Julie.

Julie
natural poet
natural as breathing

Your long black hair you tie with a squishy into a
careless bun
Your long skirts cover the tops of combat boots
When you read out loud
the ears in the room hold still
curious
catching the vibrations of your heart.

Julie wrote to me, and her word gift is one I still treasure.

Dear Mrs. Lain,

I've been a pessimist for a while now. Feeling like there is no hope, sanity or love left. I hope, now that I've been in our class, that my sour days are over. The people in this class, if they weren't too scared or inhibited, came into this class a little unknowing, but left feeling like something truly good went on this year. Something so individual that it couldn't be duplicated.

When this year is over, and it is almost, I will look back and think so sweetly of these people. I will think of the small differences we imposed at first upon each other. I am now enchanted with all people good and bad. Because, you see, there is always that last drop that makes the cup flow over with goodness. Perhaps this class is the drop I need to have my cup overflow with a little bit of Julie, a tiny bit of good that I can share in my life.
Julie.

Today Julie lives in the state of Washington where she can hear the rhythm of the ocean meeting the earth. She is working on her second book of poems.

Pure Potential

My writing friend, Emily, and I stood in my kitchen, leaning against the cupboards talking softly. She stopped by after her early morning run. Emily's skin was moist with a patina of light perspiration. A dedicated fitness freak, as she calls herself, Em's arms are solid, defying forty-plus years of gravity tugging away. Her biceps and triceps are clearly defined.

We talked about people's pure potential. Both of us have been married for thirty years, and the reason we've stayed married, in spite of all kinds of rough spots, is because Em and I are in love with people's *essence*. That's what I call it. She calls it the *core self.*

She asked me if I am bitter that my husband, Gayle, has Multiple Sclerosis, struggles with declining physical powers, faces disability.

"No, I'm not bitter." I was thinking as I talked. "At least I don't *feel* bitter."

I've thought about Gayle's disease a lot. I guess I don't care how bad he gets physically. It wasn't his exterior I loved anyway. I told her about when we first met. "When I first laid eyes on him, I stopped still in my tracks for a split second. 'So *that's* what you look like.' The thought spoke itself inside my head. 'I thought you'd be taller.'"

Em understood perfectly. "The first time I saw Osea, he had on a puke green jacket. He looked a little soft, like the Pillsbury Dough Boy." Her own biceps flexed involuntarily. "I never thought I'd marry someone so different from me."

We nodded. I told her about our car wreck, another example of how connected I feel to something *essential* about Gayle. "It was about 30 years ago. We were driving back to college our senior year. A drunk hit us as we crested a hill. I remember swimming back into consciousness a split second after the impact and asking him, 'Was it a nightmare?'"

"No," Gayle said. "It really happened. Are you hurt?"

Later, he told me that my voice got slower and slower as I listed the broken places. But I told him what he wanted to know. I told him I'd live. The first couple of weeks of my three-month hospitalization, I'd surface every few hours in a fog of pain and morphine. I was deeply comforted just knowing Gayle was sitting there. Even the pain of the crushed pelvis was bearable so long as I felt his presence.

"See," I tried to explain to Em. "See, it's Gayle's essence I love. Something inside of him. And no matter what happens to his body, whether he is confined to a wheelchair someday or bedridden, his Gayleness is what I love. So I'm not bitter. At least I don't think I am."

"I know what you mean. I call it the *core*. I love Osea's core. He's like a vitamin I need. And I say this without illusion. We've had some tough times."

Gayle has taught me a lot about what he calls pure potential. For sixteen years, he coached kids in summer baseball programs. His teams won first place so many times people lost count. For Gayle coaching meant reading the kids' strengths and capitalizing on them. He wasn't supposed to try to change kids, remaking them to fit his notions. "I like to figure out the kids' abilities, set up a situation where they can strut their stuff, and then get out of their way."

Em and I know about this inner-essence thing. We've come to realize that to really teach we have to get to know the *essence* or the *core* of every kid. Their pure potential. Em and I relate, partly because of the lessons we've learned from our marriages *and* from teaching kids.

Adrianna the Mystic

Adrianna taught me that some people are gifted with unusual perceptiveness. Writing in her journal, she shared stories. She remembered back to seventh grade, a horrible year. Adrianna sat in the principal's office more than she sat in class. The head honcho of a venomous clique, she was always in trouble, now for telling all the boys that Shelly Moench wore a new padded bra, again for smacking Colleen with a broom in home ec saying she was sick and tired of hearing Colleen whine about her mother's cancer. Insensitive and bossy, Adrianna bulldozed over people's feelings, and she wasn't happy with herself either.

She made no bones about her special intuition. Once, at her grandparents' ranch near Tie Siding, Wyoming, she bumped smack into eternity. Out on the ranch during early summer, she felt her tilted world tip upright. Climbing a rocky incline, she followed a trail of blue larkspur and mountain lupine, picking wild flowers for her grandma's oak table. She crested the hill. Suddenly, the earth fell away before her, down to a deep ravine. The view took her breath away. Something about that supercharged moment changed her. Adrianna the Tyrant was in the past.

Another time a few years later, she accepted a blind date with a kid from a neighboring town, someone whose aunt knew her mom. She didn't want to go, was late getting ready. But when she laid eyes on him standing at the front door of the living room, she stopped in her tracks, felt like she knew him before from some other time and place. They got married last summer.

Adrianna wrote in her journal about her life, marked sections for me to read, and I wrote back to her about her life-changing moments:

158

Adrianna.
Once,
time folded in on itself
and with a shiver
you felt yourself doing what you already did.
Once,
you walked out of your pink bedroom
and raised your eyes to a total stranger
and knew him.
Like Romeo and Juliet, you both knew.
Once,
you wandered through a mountain meadow growing
    gray boulders
and stepped to the brink of an earth-crack.
You felt God's breath.
You said that time is not what we think at all,
only our clutching at thin air
forcing reality to fit our puny hands.

Her standardized test scores didn't show that Adrianna was so smart, but she could read between the lines of life. In those spaces she saw much more than most of us.

Sabrina in Technicolor and Surround Sound

The first year of teaching, I felt like I didn't know what I was doing half the time, and Sabrina watched me like a hawk, missing nothing.

Sabrina was a vivid girl. Her bright red hair and violet eyes came straight out of a romance novel, but she paid scant attention to her looks. I overheard two senior boys talking about her. "It's lucky she's naturally pretty, otherwise she'd be ugly.

She never fixes herself up." That's how little attention she paid to herself — the *outside* of herself.

On the inside Sabrina's antennae, like Adrianna's, were fine-tuned, reminding me of electric wire my dad strung around the pasture to keep the cows out of the sugar beets.

She read me like a text all year. In April, when I was just beginning to suspect that I might be pregnant — maybe six or seven weeks along — she looked up at me while I was taking roll and asked, "Mrs. Lain, are you going to have a baby?" I stared at her, lost track of head counting. How did she know?

159

The First Year
Sabrina asked me,
six weeks pregnant
thin still as a 2 by 4,
"Are you pregnant?"
Her eyes followed me all year
glued
reading me more deeply than a text
I was disconcerted by her undivided attention
and hoped that since she read me unblinking
she saw enough good
to counterbalance the gaping holes, shrinking fear,
    confusion
of my first teaching job.

Sabrina had an uncanny ability to put two and two together. She was a remarkable reader, predicting plot events long before the author laid out all his clues. Likewise, she read the people around her like a clairvoyant. I often wonder if Sabrina, with her incredible powers of observation, taught me about watching students. All the better to teach them.

I use my poems to each student to validate talents already in full bloom, like David's, LaWanna's, Lisa's and Julie's. I use the power of language to help shape possibilities, however illusive and intangible, like Adrianna's and Sabrina's.

Like Gayle with his baseball boys, I see each student filing into my room as a star — those in the spotlight already and those waiting in the wings, clueless as to what they can do. They're all stars. All they need is an advocate, director, and agent wrapped up in one person. For the lucky kids, that one person might be a teacher, someone who can peer inside and see what can be. The job is difficult — make that almost impossible — considering that I am with my students less than an hour a day in a frenetic schedule, all of us bell hopping like mad for 180 days a year.

But I am working every one of those days to get a bead on my students' potential; I want to hold before their eyes an image of themselves. Maybe, then, the kids can catch a whiff of a future place where their inner selves will be fulfilled.

CHAPTER NINE

Falling Stars

AYLE'S grandpa was working in a Kansas wheat field when the *Titanic* went down. Word traveled from mouth to ear, mouth to ear, across the whole country. When the kitchen crew carried out midmorning water, they also brought news about the great disaster. Work was called off for the rest of the day out of respect for the dead.

Grandpa's body was lithe and strong back then in 1912. When he reminisced with us about the *Titanic*, he sat in a wheelchair at the old folks' home, his shoulders rounded and his dim eyes focusing on the past. I imagined that he was looking at those billowing wheat waves stretching out as far as the eye could see. The undulating motion looked like the ocean. He said he wondered what it'd be like to bob along in cold, cold water, facing death. He guessed he'd lie back and look up at the stars. He'd say goodbye to the stars, the steady stars.

Ancient navigators directed their journeys by following the lights, like the North Star, a fixed spot in space, a finger pointing the way. During my journey down the school hallways, I've known stars like LaWanna and Adrianna, and I've known falling stars, students who've lost their place in the sky. Rudderless, they plummet headlong in the night, beyond the pull of gravity to hold them steady.

I yearn for a star-catcher to arrest their downward tailspin.

DANGER! CORAL AHEAD

Some girls get stuck in the dark of their own self-loathing. Coral took one look in the mirror and hated what she saw. Actually, her relationship with herself was more like a tug of war between hate and love. Every morning she barged into the classroom, drawing all kinds of attention to herself. She was so tall! And so late. Plus she talked to herself, kept up an unceasing monologue, kind of like Robin Williams's patter-chatter, just audible enough to hear.

Most kids were scared of her, and they showed their fear by rolling their eyes. They wanted the world to know — in case anybody was looking — they were not like weird Coral. No, never that weird.

Coral didn't mind telling us and telling us what she thought — on any subject. I had my hands full curbing her a little so she didn't out-shout the other students during class discussions. The object was to let everyone speak. Coral grasped the concept, but she couldn't contain herself.

Oh, the lovely ideas she had, how beautifully she put words together! "Mrs. Lain, look at my knee. I ripped it up on Matt's skateboard — bled all over, a regular blood flood." Or, "Mrs. Lain, I'm sorry I'm late, but the hall is like a river and I was swimming upstream." Words catapulted out of her mouth and spewed from her pen. But she had trouble organizing and synthesizing all her huge ideas into some structure. Once she started to write, she couldn't discern an appropriate ending. The prose kept sprawling outward into increasingly abstract concepts. For her research topic, she chose totalitarianism, and try as we might, she couldn't narrow the subject. Somehow she wanted to capture an epic history of governments that tried to force everyone to goose step in perfect time, and then, though she never could really say so, she probably wanted to tie all this to the extrinsic controls exerted upon her by her religion and her father. She was smart, but she didn't know her own mind.

163

She wrote about her life — a tyrannical father, a submissive mother who, like Coral, followed the church's codes for womanly appearance. We never saw Coral in anything but dumpy dresses. Once, Coral unpacked her hair for us. She usually wore it wrapped around and around on top of her head. The black wave fell down to her knees. With her hair down, she looked like an exotic country and western singer.

The eldest child of six or seven kids, she both loved and loathed her role of "other mother." In spite of herself, she felt warmth flood her whole body when she held a fuzzy-headed newborn. Coral's fine artist's fingers loved the thick, elastic promise of bread dough — she made a dozen loaves a week for the family.

However, she hated her life, too: the tight constraints on her time, the chains imposed by family responsibilities and rules. In high school she exhibited some self-destructive tendencies, swiping little things from K-Mart, tempting God to see if divine retribution really worked.

Nevertheless, the troubled side of Coral wasn't my business. Instead, we had school work to shoulder, using our 44 minutes together to read and write and discuss and research.

Besides the learning, I wanted to give Coral a personal word gift, an assurance that this madcap time, this whirlpool which trapped her, might end sooner or later.

> *Coral*
> *in the mirror*
> *an embarrassed giggle*
> *caught in a whirlpool of self-loathing*
> *you exaggerate*
> *you see in the mirror's image*
> *growth gone on too long*
> *6'2" giant*
> *too big everywhere, you said.*
> *Irreconcilable our reflection and* Seventeen *perfection.*
> *Rest easy, Coral.*
> *I see beauty*
> *black hair to your knees*
> *brown eyes' wisdom*
> *When you write, words adore you.*
> *Soon enough in wider halls beyond school*
> *yours won't be the only figure to stand out.*

Last I heard, Coral was still floundering along in the cold, dark sea. She's in graduate school and therapy. I keep wishing for her rescue. Maybe, through the fog, she'll spot some stars to guide her.

DARREN THE DICTATOR

Darren's life mission was to cut himself off from human affection, mine and his classmates. Instead, he wanted control. Wrestling ownership of the classroom, he struggled with me all year. If I wouldn't grab the classroom by the throat, he would. That kind of authority he could respect. From the looks of things, once he'd gain the seat of power, he would *not* be a benevolent dictator.

In school and in life, Darren just didn't understand the concept of cooperation. Competition was his modus operandi. He lusted for power, to be king of the hill, lord of all he surveyed. Dominion came naturally to him. Ironically, his research topic for the semester was religious cults — he was fascinated with the charismatic leaders who came to an end at Waco and Guyana.

When it came time to give this boy a poem, the one I'd promised all of them, I didn't soft-soap his attempts to disrupt class. I didn't sentimentalize our relationship. He'd dismiss that fluff with a snort. Instead what I said to Darren was more a jolt than a gentle nudge.

> *Darren*
> *in my class*
> *you want to be the fulcrum*
> *the centrifugal force*
> *the eye of the tornado.*
> *You and your antihero, Jimmy Jones,*
> *want to create the world in your own image.*
> *Then we'll be happy little followers holding Dixie cups*
> *   of red Koolaid*
> *laced with arsenic.*
> *You wrestle with me every day.*
> *At least it keeps my muscles toned.*

At the end of the year, a few of Darren's classmates alluded to him in their reflections, suggesting that the class melded in spite of *The Big D*. I felt sorry for the boy, foreseeing a future of ill-fitting communities filled with people he'd blame when they refused to follow him. Darren occupied a very lonely place at the bull's eye of his own universe.

Jacob the Couch Potato

While some boys like Darren the Dictator tried to raise Cain in the classroom, isolating themselves at the top of the heap, some others like Jacob withdrew, glazed over by television, an addiction for Jacob that took the place of real adventure, friends and games to play. I wrote him this poem to see if I could get any life out of him. It was a wake-up call: "Yoo, hoo, Jacob! Are you in there?"

Jake
babied into passivity
you seem content to rule
the fake domain of TV land.
If one program bores you
press the button
erase its existence.
Couch King,
you summon
jesters from "Saturday Night Live"
troubadours on MTV
jousters of NFL.
All your experiences are vicarious.
From your recliner
how can you know
the cold shock of adventure,

leaping bare naked into Crow Creek Reservoir
and afterward toweling away gooseflesh?

Prodding Jacob didn't work. He was too sluggish to turn in a single assignment. I called in his dad to see what we could do to wake up the boy, get him learning and passing. The father told me the story. When Jacob was ten years old, his mom contracted liver cancer. During her bedridden year before the welcome arms of death, Jacob waited on her hand and foot. He skipped being a typical fourth and fifth grader. Skipped entirely all the natural naughty stages. Jacob's dad figured his son made some kind of mental deal with God that he'd be very, very good if only.... Neither of us knew what to do to jar Jacob out of his long convalescence.

Jacob had reasons for burying himself in cotton-ball numbness. Not all my students had Jacob's excuse for tuning out.

ALAN LOVED TO HATE

Alan hated me, from the first day of school. He wasn't passive, like Jacob. He actively stoked the fire of this lovely, hot rage. I don't know why. Maybe he loathed English on general principles. Or maybe he saw me as soft and vulnerable and decided I'd be a safe target. I knew his mom. I'd heard her complain about schools, the indifferent office staffs, unprofessional teachers. Perhaps she inadvertently set him up. In her dinnertime tirades, he heard permission to blame schools for his own lack of cooperation.

Leaving school one day, I wove my way through the cars and potholes in the parking lot. Alan's vehicle and mine met nose to nose. Recognizing him, I smiled and backed up a little, waving him on. Alan and the guy with him wore sunglasses, the kind that reflect like chrome. "Bitch!" He mouthed the word, big as life, his fly eyes looking straight through me. I'd smiled at him before his message registered.

I gave this poem to Alan. Forget sugar coating. He'd throw the poem away if it slouched away from the truth between us. Come to think of it, he probably pitched it out anyway.

> *Alan,*
> *I am not a bitch!*
> *I read your lips shaping the word*
> *"Bitch"*
> *for your companion*
> *sitting in the high seat of the parked pickup*
> *sunglasses and chrome reflecting me*
> *so cool.*
> *Before my brain registered the insult*
> *I'd smiled at you*
> *in greeting.*
> *Now your sunglasses mirror*
> *my crooked smile*
> *slipping sideways down my face.*

No matter how immune I grow to kids' middle fingers drilling the air, hostility like Alan's feels like a hot lava spill. When I gave Alan the poem, his face showed no reaction. He did read it, though. That's something.

PHILLIP, THE COOL DUDE

Often the students in my room seem perched on the edge of things, like birds on an overhead wire, ready to flit away.

They seem unwilling to ground themselves long enough for any of this schooling stuff to sink in. School, with students hurrying from class to class, different subjects, bells marking off the time, exacerbate their unconnectedness.

Phillip Ortiz was adrift. Toward me, his classmates and the work of the classroom, he was aloof as a cat. In tenth grade his dad kicked him out of the house. They had a knockdown drag-out. I think because Phillip was hanging out with druggies. So Phillip, new tattoo and all, slept on the couch at his older brother's place, a shaky sanctuary. For two months at the beginning of tenth grade, he wore sunglasses in class and hid out at the end of the row, dozing.

Phillip wasn't ever completely gone, though. He joined class discussions, whenever we had them, so, just to keep him alert, I'd occasionally start class with a philosophical question, like whether the students bought into Kohlberg's hierarchy of moral reasoning. "Do some people behave just because they're afraid of being punished? Are others good because they believe that all humankind, including themselves, will benefit?"

Phillip perked up every time he heard such open-ended questions, clearing his throat to speak. I gave Phillip this poem after he started smiling at me with one side of his mouth. I hoped he'd see I wanted him with us in this learning place.

Phillip
pull off those glasses.
Why are you hiding behind shades?
Are you testing the water in here
still maintaining some degree of defiance?
Are you trying to show us how expensive they are?
Are you trying to sleep?
Social convention says, "Pull off the glasses.

They block eye-to-eye communication."
Well, sunglasses make a statement
communicate, too, right?
But once we get the message, then
will you take them off?

Later, Phillip earned his dad's approval and he moved back home. Wrestling season rolled around. He put himself on a diet and quit smelling like cigarettes. I remember the diet because on days he had to weigh in, he carried a cup to spit in. Said he planned to drop some water weight.

In eleventh grade, I didn't have Phillip in class, but he came by once in a while. One spring day, the school reeled with the news that Miguel, a recent graduate, had been murdered, shot to death just when he was finishing his finals over at the University of Wyoming. Phillip and I were especially wounded. Miguel was a friend of Phillip's and a star student of mine. We pinned our hopes on Miguel, hoping he'd point the way so other West Side kids could reach up and grasp the golden ring.

When Phillip heard the news, he appeared at my door. We put our arms around each other and cried. He wasn't hiding behind sunglasses that day.

JUMPING OFF

Like in a dream of falling, Phillip awoke before he hit bottom. I watched so many students settle into orbit, only to zing off again, leaping into unknown territory. Makes me wonder if taking risks is a chronic human urge. Even I, the human chicken, learned about jumping, and the lessons served me well during a career of teaching secondary school. It's risky to step out into thin air, no clear cut direction, no guarantees, even when the old ways are so wrong for kids.

When I was nine years old, our landlocked farming town got a new indoor swimming pool. I spent hours there. I liked swimming underwater. With my eyes shut, I'd imagine my body moving through pale green silk. A high school girl in the fifties had no sports to compete in. Synchronized swimming was sport enough. So with the rest of the girls, I swam, holding huge lung-fulls of air while we performed a kaleidoscope of patterns underwater. Together our bodies scissored and arched, resembling flowers opening first one way and then another.

I swam, but I was afraid to dive. I could not bring my toes to release their hold on the lip of the high dive even though my girlfriend, Sheila, pressed me forward, begging me to hurry up and jump. The first few times on that high, thin line in the air, I had to retreat down the ladder, my tail between my legs. All the goose bumpy kids, strung up the rungs, groaned as they stepped backward to release me from my fear.

The next time up, I took Sheila with me, out to the very edge of the world. "Push me when I'm ready," I told her, and she obliged.

Four years later, I had to relearn this same jumping lesson. Every once in a while, a school office messenger would deliver a note to my classroom. The teacher would walk down the long row to my desk and put the little slip in front of me. I'd open it and read: "Your mother called. Take the Garland bus tonight." The words had the power to awaken all my school-dulled cells. I could feel my heart spread its wings with joy. That's how much I loved going to my grandparents' farm. So when my aunt Donna, three years ahead of me, invited me to her hay ride party, I was really happy.

Grandpa drove the little Ford tractor pulling the wagon full of noisy kids roughhousing in the mounds of hay. I could see his silhouette against the setting sun. He braked on the bluffs overlooking the homestead. Then he left us to our fun, returning when the moon was two hours higher in the sky.

First, we roasted wieners and marshmallows. After eating food, enhanced by the flavor of char, the boys sought adventure. Orin sized up the distance from the overhanging lip of the sandstone cliff to the sandy bed below. He allowed as how jumping would be a safe thrill. Screaming and shouting, their voices sparking with excitement, kids began leaping off sandstone cliffs into beds of sand below. In the bright night, illumined by stars and a moon big as a barn door, kids jumped, the bravest ones first. No one broke a thing, not a neck or a shoelace. But I just couldn't bring myself to jump. Not even to show off for the high schoolers.

At the age of 24, I did take a leap into my first teaching job. At the time, I thought it was a safe enough move, Wind River High being only a hundred miles away. But compared to my home town, the Wind River Indian Reservation might as well have been a foreign country. Where I grew up, Elvis gyrating on *The Ed Sullivan Show* was a big deal. On the reservation, a big deal was much bigger.

I stepped into the classroom. My eyes felt like squinting, like the time I stepped out of Wind Cave into merciless sunlight. The view from the perspective of the teacher's desk stopped me up short. All those faces formed a sort of chaotic jumble. Sixty percent of the students were white — offspring of hardworking farmers who owned or leased land nearby. They seemed familiar enough, like kids back home. But the other forty percent were Native American, Shoshone and Arapaho. Those were the ones who taught me the most.

For instance, I tend to touch people. When I touched Dana Smith, the Assembly of God minister's daughter, she smiled, her forehead unfurrowing. But when I rested my fingers on Amado's shoulder—a ninth-grade Arapaho—his pores froze and his skin's message was as loud as a command: "Don't touch me!"

Those kids had plenty of reasons not to trust me or the school culture. Almost everything we did went against the grain. Standing up in the front of the room giving speeches felt like showing off. Using eye contact was as disrespectful as giving people the finger. Reading in the *Adventures of American Literature* anthology about Manifest Destiny and achieving the American Dream felt like somebody else's victory. No wonder those kids slumped at their desks and eventually quit coming. No wonder they jumped blind into uncalculated dangers.

AMADO LEAPS INTO BLACK HOLES

Amado was like Jacob. Both sought seductive short cuts which lured them into dead ends. Instead of coming to grips with life, as capricious and cruel as it seemed to be, they found anesthesia. Jacob's was television. Amado's was another kind of mind alteration.

Some of my Native American students, like Amado, whipped themselves into a frenzy. As if a virus were in the air, the boys caught suicide sickness, playing with nooses in their basements. Amado was one of the boys who survived all kinds of crazy tricks to get high, including oxygen deprivation and glue inhalation.

Amado
where are your tree houses
perched on outstretched arms lifting
hosannas to the sky?

Where are your joys tied on flying kite tails
of boyhood?
Our species has come to such a state
when boys like you
who once raced bareback on painted ponies
black hair flailing side to side
seek highs
sniffing glue
and playing death tag in the basement with a noose.

174

Three years after I quit teaching at Wind River High School, I found Amado's name in the newspaper — not in the obituaries, but the police blotter. He was arrested for knifing some guy, another Native American, in the K Bar. The news felt like a knife-thrust to my heart.

ANGELA FLEW THE COOP

In the fall of her ninth-grade year, Angela was desperate. I thought she looked like those darling round-faced, curly-headed girls portrayed in Mother Goose illustrations; she thought she looked fat. A boy, her locker neighbor, had yelled, "Move your fat ass." That clinched it. She became obsessed with dieting, losing and gaining, losing and gaining.

Besides the weight thing, her popularity quotient didn't register high enough to suit her, partly because she flitted from group to group like a bee, trying to please everyone. For a while, to be popular she went to parties, got drunk, and made a fool out of herself. That didn't work and she hated herself even more.

In April, Angela decided to run away from home. She was gone a week, sleeping in a camper trailer parked in a friend's back yard, unbeknownst to the owners of the camper. Laura, her girlfriend, fed her leftovers from her house. Angela slept or sat and thought. It wasn't much fun after the second day. Inside that little camper—cold at night and hot otherwise—the hours lost their definition. Sameness redefined boredom. Finally, she opened the door and walked home, in need of a shower and shampoo.

For a whole month she wrote nonstop about her leap into the unknown. I wrote this poem back to her.

Angela
at first, running away
is giddy lightness
free flight moon gravity
freedom to be nobody or somebody else
later
it's free fall tumbling in a vacuum
finally
it's who am I
and too much like dying.
May I come back now?

Undaunted by her first flight, Angela kept trying her wings. She dyed her blonde hair purple and gave herself a new style—little spikes pointing straight off her head. Her ensemble included black eye shadow, maroon, almost black, lipstick, and baggy, black clothes that hid her whole body. With her Statue of Liberty persona, she seemed happier. Once, a friend told me that when she sees these kids with their bizarre get-ups, she doesn't worry about them any more. They are broadcasting, "Hey, I am me. Live with it!"

After Angela returned, the class read *Romeo and Juliet*. When the play opens, Romeo is moping around. I asked the kids if they thought Romeo was depressed, quoting the lines about him locked in his room, "making an artificial night," and about the chaos of mixed sensations — hotness and coldness, the trembling and not trembling, the two halves of peace and despair rubbing against each other. Angela nodded her head. She seemed to learn more from Romeo about getting her bearings, about the human condition of cluelessness, than she did from my advice. Learning was healing for her — all that connecting, discussing, probing, wondering, wrestling with contradiction, and solving problems. Like Grandma did with her eggs, she held her ideas up against the light to check to see if they were fertile.

SANDY THE ZIT PICKER

First semester, Sandy drove me nuts. She pressed against boundaries, testing the edges of propriety and teacher patience. She picked every rule or guideline and scraped them bloody, even the most elastic ones. Every time I made an assignment, she asked, "Why? What good would it do?" And when she had all the reasons explained, she'd overanalyze the assignments, leaving the whole thing a lifeless carcass in the middle of the room. After explaining the work, I took to ignoring her waving hand. She looked like an angel with her blond head of hair and eyes the color of wild irises, but if I'd call on her, she'd harass the assignment to death. In November, I wrote her a curt little poem.

Nit Picking
Pink fingernail
a crowbar

stained
a bloody memorial
to pried-off zits, warts
skin not yet ready to shuck
picking, picking the puckered scab
until the final tender tear
never leaving well enough alone.

Sandy's eyes skipped across the lines, down the poem, devouring the words. One eyebrow lifted and the side of her mouth angled upwards—a rueful sort of expression. Then she shrugged and threw the paper in her rat's nest of a backpack, a casually defiant dismissal. She kept up her jack-hammering in class, right to the end of the semester. I was heated enough to write another little edgy piece.

Sandy
refuses every rule.
You snorted today, just audibly.
You'd asked to use the bathroom,
and I said, "Take the pass."
You consider
rules ludicrous.
Sandy.
Some rules are required
to stretch us,
calisthenics of growth.
We need them to break.
When none are imposed,
we have no tension,
like a stretched rubber band,
to propel us forward.

To her credit Sandy overlooked my own nit-picking preachiness and wrote me back.

Dear Mrs. Lain,
    Thanks for the poems. You know us really well. I respect that you took the time.

Second semester, Sandy wrote a lot of poetry, often modeling her poems on those I'd read out loud at the beginning of class. Like nothing else, poetry electrifies the air of the classroom. The high-voltage words have enough piercing power to get to the soft centers of even the most callused kids like Sandy. Her poem told me *why* she was a scab-picker.

Some Girls Are Untouchable

Langston Hughes said
that a dream deferred
would
explode
but, Oh, Langston,
have you lived too little
or have you loved too much?
Let me tell you about my dream deferred
I was a promising young girl
Skinny legs
tiny red lips
golden hair
untouched hips
so violently forced
to grow up.
My dreams

were of daisychains, milkmaids,
holding hands and kissing
at midnight's door step
so violently forced
to grow up.
Oh, I became the untouchable
My dream deferred
imploded
unlike you ... I
have lived too much
to be so young
and loved too little
to be so old.
I ask you this,
Dear Langston:
Will I explode?
Will I explode?
Will I explode?

No wonder she rubbed everyone raw.

Sandy felt her way down the corridors of high school. She took classes like psychology, humanities, and composition, and she entered into a dialogue with scholars whose big ideas helped her work out the kinks in her life. Reading and writing and studying gave Sandy a key to open her mind and heal her heart.

CHRIS — SCARED SILLY

While some kids like Amado and Melissa jump into mid-air, Chris's mind gripped the narrowest ledge of ideas. He wanted to have everything nailed down. If he kept school boxed in a little container, it wouldn't be too heavy to carry around, wouldn't rattle his cage much. He hankered for complacency. I suspect the reason for his compulsion to trivialize every assignment, to ignore anything abstract, rested in fear of losing his handhold on the high trapeze, and maybe fear of hard work. I chided Chris about his unwillingness to sink his teeth into meaty issues. His stock answer in class discussions was, "I don't know." My poem to Chris turned out to be a warning.

> *Chris*
> *you come down to every bottom line.*
> *What is the bottom line, you ask and ask,*
> *seeking labels to store and later drop*
> *with faked innocence,*
> *weapons in your arsenal*
> *stacked up on the shelf of the bottom line.*
> *Whoa, Chris!*
> *Even the bottom line is slippery*
> *slimy with green moss.*
> *Sharp coral teeth*
> *and serrated spears of shattered glass*
> *wait to slice your white toes,*
> *turning water red.*
> *Look down at your feet through layers of water*
>   *wrinkles.*
> *See them move along the bottom line?*
> *Any moment it may drop off*
> *into a dark water abyss.*
> *Unnamed creatures sleep there.*
> *Once aroused, they sting,*
> *spring away the pseudo-secure bottom line.*
> *Where is this so-called bottom line to cling to?*

Research paper time rolled around. At first, Chris folded his arms across his chest. "I don't want to probe, wonder, analyze." His body language scowled. He wanted to avoid the deep thinking, the hard work of forging connections between the ideas in books and the practice of his daily life. But little by little, as the year progressed, he swung out, a little farther each time, from his secure mole hole in the back row.

Spirituality engrossed him. Sioux Indian style. At the end of the research project, his reflective letter explained why he'd picked his topic, commented on all he'd learned, and peered into his own learning styles. He gained insight into the evolution of his thinking. In this letter, he mentioned that his favorite piece of writing was the short story. Ironic. He'd given me all kinds of hassle about my assignment to write a creative research paper, requiring a piece of fiction or a poem to accompany the traditional research. "Why can't we just do a straight research paper? I already know how to do that. Why do you have to make something up? I don't even know how to write a story." These were his early whinings. His reflection shows that he changed his mind:

Dear Mrs. Lain,

My paper was, like most composition papers, a great deal of work. However, unlike most papers I have written in the past I enjoyed this one. Many weekend nights I would go out and spend the entire night thinking of ideas for my paper and wanting to get back home to write them down. I would come home at twelve and start typing.

The research part of the paper was of course the least enjoyable for me. Although I learned a great deal of information on my topic, I didn't enjoy the work. The part of my paper that was so enjoyable was the story. I loved creating and writing it. The literary analysis was difficult too, but I enjoyed reading the books, so writing about them was no problem. I have not done my presentation yet, but I have my ideas. My dad has his own tapes of the Custer Battlefield. I am thinking of showing these along with "Son of the Morning Star." Combining them would show the land and the story.

This year of composition was the most work I have ever put into a class. At the beginning of the year I hated the class and felt the work was too difficult. I am so glad now I took the class, I no longer am scared of writing papers.

Sincerely,

Chris

Chris's change of heart makes for a happy teacher story, something we all hope for. The curriculum reached out and grabbed Chris, arresting his downward spiral and making a difference to him as a learner.

Enrique the Pigeonholer

Enrique was like Chris, only he didn't let loose as long as I knew him. All year he clung to the narrow confines of his old beliefs like a treed cat too scared to come down.

I suppose it's human nature to look for black-and-white answers. Enrique wanted simple worksheets with clear-cut rights and wrongs. It drove him to distraction to have to read student writing and critique it. Maybe he sensed that Weldon's piece, with all its misspellings, was more riveting than Rachel's piece with all those straight margins and perfectly punctuated sentences, but he didn't want to analyze that hard to see why one piece worked and another didn't. He'd just shrug his shoulders and put "nice writing" on Rachel's and circle the misspelled words on Weldon's. Enrique was a competent spellcheck, but a lazy critic.

What bothered me about Enrique was his hard-line labeling and casual dismissing of people. Like a smug little god, his word was law. I got fed up with his neat little tags for everyone, his reductionistic attitude about people and learning. So I wrote to him. Remembering my Spanish, I found myself wishing that our language, too, had a more conditional verb for IS:

> *Enrique,*
> *IS*
> *is an innocent looking word,*
> *but IS*
> *is evil.*
> *"She IS*
> *fat ugly bitch.*
> *He IS fag.*
> *Enrique, IS circumscribes*
> *imprisons.*
> *No self-respecting verb should sit in stolid judgment.*
> *At least the Spanish have Esta — the momentary IS.*

Probably, Enrique's efforts to box, seal and label everyone and everything served to help him get a handle on the universe, find some patterns so he could make sense and navigate his way. That's understandable. I hoped, though, that I might nudge him, so that someday he could get a little more comfortable with the unclassifiable, the unpredictable.

Marissa's Homesickness

Marissa was homesick.

Ours is a transient society and Cheyenne is no exception. With F. E. Warren Air Force Base here, some students move in and out of school following their parents' military careers. Other kids move to town from the farm. Such was Marissa's case. She wrote all the time about trying to make a home away from home.

For the first few months, her writing notebook wept in my hands. I collected these spiral notebooks every couple of weeks to tally pages of drafts, check to see if students were applying the class mini-lessons in their rough drafts, and skim their reading notes. Barely into chapter two of *To Kill a Mockingbird*, Marissa reflected on Scout's sense of home. She said she was jealous that Scout had a place like that, a dependable place. "Growing up is changeable enough," she wrote.

We talked after school one day. She'd volunteered to come in and help assemble the class literary magazine. "I've been homesick all my life," I told her. "I don't think about it all the time, but every once in a while, a certain gust of wind will lift my skirt a little just the way it did that day when I stepped outside my high school. It was my sixteenth birthday. I guess that's why I remember that pure feeling of exhilaration."

Marissa remembered home feelings, too. She talked about them. About how she used to climb into the irrigation ditches in early spring, before they let the water down, and burrow into a tunnel she made under the tumbleweeds. I asked her if she ever raced herself to see if she could hold her breath running from one end of the corral fence to the other. I'd do that, I told her, so I wouldn't have to breathe in the hot smell of cow manure and silage. Marissa grinned at how silly we were as kids on the farm. She told me about lying down in an alfalfa field and listening to the plants grow.

"When I moved here from Riverton," I told her, "the thing I noticed most was how no one knew me in the grocery store." She nodded her head, her eyebrows lifted in agreement. We knew what it was like to be in a place where everybody knew everybody. Later, I jotted Marissa a little note in her spiral about the pain of moving.

Marissa
In the hallway
your frantic eyes scan
the lines of faces
for one familiar one.
Your eyes can't help it
They dart about
looking for a Face
opening into smiling reflection.

In our classroom, we read about characters who felt cut off, like Ray Bradbury's Montag when he broke from the rest of the firemen in the novel *Fahrenheit 451*. Marissa saw her life theme reflected in fictional people whose lives seemed more real sometimes than her own. She was comforted to know that loneliness and homesickness are themes for everybody, period. Besides reading about this feeling of rootlessness, she wrote about it. Marissa's descriptive writing was as potent as picante sauce when she revisited her memories of the hiding place under the tumbleweeds. For some students, like Marissa and Sandy, learning can be a lighthouse.

Unlike the falling stars of the heavens, the downward trajectory of the students I've described here is not inevitable. Some have reversed their descent, aided by talent, luck, circumstances and, perhaps, a caring teacher and a poem.

CHAPTER TEN

Heroes

M Y second son, Tagg, is a grown man, an English teacher and a coach. He has a passion and a knack for leading boys through the intricacies of basketball, track and baseball. "I'm a shaper of men." He laughed out loud at how much his words sounded like bragging. But he was feeling expansive. His boys had just taken first in state.

I taught this son when he was a seventh grader. The school computer sorted him into my classroom. "Should I throw him back?" I asked some of his former teachers. They thought he'd be no problem for me, so I kept him. I'm glad, because seeing my teaching from his point of view taught me lesson after lesson.

The other evening he came by the house.

"Mom." I quit peeling carrots and looked up. "Remember the lift you got working with those journalism kids after school?" He was reminding me of the hours the seventh graders and I spent making a school newspaper. We were a team, laughing together, creating and solving all kinds of problems. "Well, you should've coached. I get that potent feeling a lot, coaching."

He was right. I yearned for potency in the classroom. I needed an antidote to the hordes of chattering human beings who raced pell-mell in and out the door, paying scant attention to reading and writing. In their wake, I felt like I needed spiritual vitamins. But during those after-school hours, students bent over the light table rearranging page layouts: *that* work was fulfilling. Like Tagg's young athletes, these kids listened as if their lives depended on it.

How can a teacher take 28 kids and hush their mouths long enough to give them a lift comparable to Tagg's championship basketball team, all the arms and legs chugging like pistons in synch as if they're choreographed?

I've learned that the best way to create the classroom community I'm after is to connect with students one at a time. That's why I wrote poems to kids — they powered-up the teaching and learning in my room. When I put a poem in the palm of a kid's hand, his ears perked up, just like our quarter horse Storm's do when he hears the oats rattling in the rusty coffee can. The ears of the whole class stood at attention. In the quiet of such intense listening, I heard the pulse of the room. For some reason, after the poems, students began to place a higher value on words. I know they saved these word snippets. They've told me so years later, maybe standing in line for a movie at the mall. "Hey, Mrs. Lain. Remember that poem you wrote? I still got it. Saved the whole kit and caboodle."

Kyle at Full Volume

Over the years, as I've written a poem for every student, I've come to see some of them as heroes.

Being a hero isn't always romantic — like taking a bullet for someone else, or feeding a starving child instead of yourself. Instead, heroism is making life count. Wringing memories out of dull, everyday moments.

Though being heroic never crossed ninth-grade Kyle's mind, he was a hero. He threaded his way through the tricky minefields of adolescence without the guidance of a father, and he excelled, deciding to play the game of life to the hilt. Kyle's humor enlivened us all, always a joke on the tip of his tongue. Even Jacob stirred to life a little when Kyle danced into class. Kyle was a master at using humor to wake us all up.

"Knock, knock."

"Who's there?"

"Butch, Jimmy and Joe."

"Butch, Jimmy and Joe who?"

"Butch your arms around me, Jimmy a kiss and let's Joe home."

One day we were all lifeless. I told the class I'd read a study saying that we can trick our bodies into being deliciously aware, thus happy. We have to do three things: pull our cheeks up into a grin, however fake, expel puffs of air from our bellies in pseudo belly laughs, and walk fast. We went outside and tried it, with Kyle as our walking leader. We looked like a drunken marching band following our drum major. Maybe the research was true; we all laughed. After we settled into our seats, everyone got to work, lips turned up instead of flat.

Kyle's single-parent mom worked at Albertsons. I've shopped there 16 years, and for almost that long she's checked out my groceries. I gave him this poem, a tribute to his spunkiness.

189

Kyle's a good boy, smart.
He was named student of the month
and invited me down to the honorary breakfast.
He's warm-eyed and smiles with a sweetness still
in spite of rib-cracking hall bullies.
After he lost the student council election,
he announced to the class, "I'm such a loser,"
just to clear the air,
in case anyone didn't vote for him.
No hard feelings
This kid is no loser.
He's hard-core evidence a latchkey kid,
mom holding down three jobs,
can waterslide laughing down the shoot.

THE JAMES PUTS ONE FOOT AHEAD OF THE OTHER

Sometimes heroism is just surviving. Making it from here to there. That's what James did. He was a sophomore. His dad was in the military so James was new in town, living in temporary quarters until they could find a place. Chronic asthma thinned him out so that he looked about ten years old. He had plenty of pluck and the confidence that things would turn out all right. He made friends with another new kid, Buddy. Sometimes they hung out in the periphery of my room, never taking center stage, but feeling at home. James would be fine sooner or later, once he gained a little maturity. I wrote this for him at Christmas. We'd just finished reading a story he liked, "The Scarlet Ibis," about a very exotic bird which landed by happenstance on alien shores. I guessed he could relate to the ibis, moving as he did from California to cold, windy Cheyenne. I wanted to tell James he, too, was a rare bird, a brave young man.

> *James*
> *You remind me sometimes*
> *of a poster child:*
> *"For pennies a day, adopt this child,"*
> *with your large brown eyes often underlined in blue*
>   *bruises of illness.*
> *My heart softens,*
> *not in pity*
> *for you have courage,*
> *you Scarlet Ibis boy,*
> *a very rare breed of bird*
> *trapped here in this cold, unfriendly climate.*
> *You dutifully fulfill student functions,*
> *even though the desk does not fit your small frame,*
> *and wait for hormones to click in*
> *and maturity to offer strength.*

191

"The James," as he called himself, read the poem over, wondering just what I meant. He went back and reread. He looked up at me. I was smiling, so he must have figured I wasn't trying to insult him. He read again, this time squinting to see between the lines. He wrote me this on-the-spot note:

> *Dear Mrs. Lain,*
>   *Thanks for the poem! At first I though it was going to be insulting. But now after I think about it, I see you are right.*
> *The James*

He got the message and stayed on track. By the time James was a senior, he wasn't a boy anymore. He'd filled out and began to carry himself with resoluteness. I don't know where he is today, but I bet he's dealing with life just fine, one day at a time.

Rex Won't Be Pinned

Rex didn't dream of being heroic, but he was indomitable. Once I watched him wrestle an older boy in a junior high wrestling match. His opponent took early advantage, had Rex in a pinning combination before Rex knew what hit him. Refusing to be pinned, he held himself in a cradle for two excruciating minutes, blood dripping from his nose into his eyes. This same heroic doggedness saved his dad's life.

> *Rex,*
> *every November weekend you go hunting with your*
> *   dad.*
> *Last weekend a wild bullet from some hunter*
> *ricocheted off a nearby rock*
> *and struck your father in the face.*
> *Both of you were sitting like lizards on gray stones*
> *warming in the sun.*
> *The bullet knocked him from his comfort.*
> *You didn't notice, eyes glued to a spotting scope scanning*
> *   the valley below.*
> *"What hit me?"*
> *Dad could still wonder,*
> *so he wasn't dead.*
> *But he couldn't see.*

His fingers explored his face,
not knowing what they'd find.
Meanwhile, you sat there unknowing.
"Rex, don't turn around."
He still wanted to protect you from the truth.
"Just listen.
I'm hurt.
My face.
My eyes.
Can't see.
Don't look!
Just help me up. Lead me to the truck. Can you?
I'll put my hand right here on your shoulder.
Can you find the way back?
Remember the stream?
Follow it west into the sun."
You led,
hiked an hour, silent.
"Dad, I can stand to look now. I need to know how
    bad."
You looked unblinking at his shattered cheekbone.
The bullet entered the eyebrow
behind one eye and out
the bridge of the nose.
Resolute in the face of blood and reshapen familiarity,
you say,
"Your face looks good, Dad.
Your left eye untouched.
Let's go to the doctor."
And you led again down into the moon-drenched
    meadow,

193

guiding feet over fallen timber and around boulders old
    as stars.
He shadowed every step
to the pickup.
Without a license,
you took your turn being father
and piloted him to safety.

Rex got his dad to the doctor, and Dewie's face was reconstructed. Is it any surprise that this boy, who didn't lose his cool when his dad was shot, became a national champion wrestler in college?

The James and Rex both show that heroism is sometimes just putting one foot in front of the other, no matter what. The discipline of sticking to something over the long haul — a career, a marriage, a wrestling goal — teaches all of us about ourselves.

DANA CAME OUT

Dana felt different, and the students, sensing her difference, felt awkward around her. It was written in their aloofness, their faces a battleground, torn between kindness and wariness.

Being different disappointed and depressed Dana, but she found ways to live with herself. Dana was short, stocky, a tree trunk of a girl, thick skin and all. Her hair was black, cut short and moussed spiky. Every day she wore a black leather jacket and jeans. Her only jewelry was a necklace, a chain of little round b-b's, like the pull chain on the attic light. The ornament was a yin-yang symbol, a white dot inside the black, a black dot inside the white, the two shapes resembling baby embryos.

One of Dana's passions was karate. She casually mentioned one day she had a black belt. I knew just enough about martial arts to realize a black belt translated into years of training, physical work and mental discipline.

Writing, though, was not her forte. Her handwriting was cramped tight, small hieroglyphics, painfully hard for me to read. The print was so embedded into the journal paper that I could almost read the message on the blank page underneath. As a writer she was stymied.

Little by little she unzipped her jacket and her mind. The timed writings helped. I started with five minutes.

"Write. The only rule is keep moving that hand for five minutes. Something will emerge. Write everything you know about ... fudge. What do you remember about ... trees. Just write, even when your mind balks, talks back, tries to shut you down. Just write over and over, I remember ... I remember ... until you do remember something. Remember, you're just limbering up your mind, like a runner who stretches out before his run. He braces against the wall and, with one leg behind the other, he leans into the solidness, stretching his calf muscles, his Achilles. Swimmers practice deep, deep breathing until they hold huge balloons of air. Actors do it, stalking the empty stage, vocalizing nonsense, limbering up their vocal cords. Writing practice loosens you up, too, gets you past your bossy, daytime mind, the one that keeps lists and orders you around."

One day, Dana's writing exploded. Her handwriting cutting loose into round circles. At first, I wondered if someone else were writing in her journal for her. She wrote about her yin yang symbol, how black proves there's white.

Though Dana was uncomfortable at school, she loved her part-time job at a nursing home. Those old people at the tail end of their lives didn't know that Dana felt like a goose in a flock of ducks. As the year went on, her word sketches about her patients became increasingly visual, their bright eyes peering out of her journal, their faces crumpled like the paper Dana rolled around and around in her hands until it was soft as Kleenex.

I wrote to Dana alluding to her divergence, a piece meant to recognize her heroism and give solace.

Labels
Smug, omnipotent words.
Sever head from heart,
squirting blood pumping the body dry.
Eyes narrowed
the judge measures a black coffin.
Death by definition.
I asked my lesbian friend once
why her childhood's religion rejected her.
She drew a circle on my counter top with her finger,
the same finger others point at her back.
"This is a closed system.
It allows no new ideas in.
Any closed system is a pressure cooker ready to explode."
Take heart, Dana.
While angels danced correctly on the head of a pin
Galileo pointed skyward.
Yes, the church slammed its stained glass window,
but the glass cracked anyway.
And Columbus didn't sail off the edge of blue.

And Spaniard politician priests who fired up all those
     heretics
added more light to read in the night.
Too much convergence explodes.
The frontal lobes work in concentric circles, widening.
Once the circle closes, beware, Label Maker!
Short circuits,
death by electrocution.
FDA! Mark a skull and crossbones
Surgeon General! Mark labels as hazardous to health.
English teachers! With red marks, ban their use.

I wanted to show Dana that her particular journey with all its baggage was difficult, but history gives us a perspective that is comforting. We aren't really all alone here, forging ahead where no one has ever been.

Sometimes being a hero means finding a lifeboat and hanging on for dear life, like Dana did with her karate, her job and her yin-yang symbol.

GABE, AN UNLIKELY ANGEL

Gabe defied my attempts to pigeonhole him. Just when I thought I had him pinned down, he transmuted on me. He "morphed," as my Trekkie students would have said.

Gabe, short for Gabriel, a transfer student from Florida, defied being classified. After the poetry genre study, the students wrote and discussed the lessons they learned from the poems as they connected this literature to their own lives. Chris Spritzler said she knew close up how bad it is to be pegged as "deviant" and then persecuted. Her uncle recently came out of the closet, married his partner. Later, the uncle and niece talked long into the night about the pain and joy of his life.

Gabe freaked about Chris's casual acceptance of her uncle's divergent lifestyle. He blushed to the roots of his hair and could not hold his tongue. "That's disgustin'!" Evidently the word "homosexual" was taboo where he came from, and now Chris Spritzler actually said out loud she condoned "it," her uncle being "one" and all.

"You're homophobic!" Chris was mad, called Gabe hopelessly prejudiced. I walked over and put my hand on Chris's rigid shoulder to calm her.

One day, though, I discovered that this boy, so easy to categorize as a pig-headed bigot, was also an angel. It happened on the day my back went out, right in the middle of a poetry read-around.

The old familiar pain struck, this time so intensely I couldn't walk. Hard as I tried to resist the pull of gravity, I couldn't stand up any longer. So I laid down right on the floor of the class. Seemingly nonplused, the sophomores circled up around me to finish their read-aloud. Tom directed traffic, calling on people. Everyone cooperated, and the class never missed a beat. I figured I'd get through these minutes before the bell and then whatever, an ambulance, a gurney, a divine miracle.

The bell rang. The kids wondered what to do with me, but they all left. All except Gabe. He knelt by me. "Mrs. Lain, I'll get you up. I won't pull you, but if you'll just take a hold of my arm here, I'll brace you as you pull. Come on, now. You can do it."

I trusted him. Something — his faith, my predicament — gave me the courage to try. I tested the strength of his arm and body anchoring me. He held firm, and gradually I stood upright. As I hobbled to the phone, he turned and left. Didn't even ask for a pass to excuse his tardiness.

When I gave him this poem, he was completely embarrassed. "Mrs. Lain?" The class was now empty. "I want to ask you a favor, Ma'am. Please don't mention that I helped you up again. OK?" I guess he wanted me to keep a lid on it so he could cultivate a tough-guy image at school, probably out of self-defense.

Gabe transferred in from Florida.
His accent's so thick,
sounds like his tongue's kneading bread dough.
"This is English?" he asked incredulous.
His previous class was strict grammar tests and dia-
*   gramming sentences.*
During a heated class discussion about homosexuality
and everyone's right to be different,
Gabe blushed and disagreed.
"Mrs. Lain, y'all are so liberal here,"
he drawled, when the room was empty.
One day my back went out.
Pain pulled me
prone on the floor.
If I could just lie down
maybe I could last until the bell.
After milling around like nervous sheep,
the kids followed habit out the door.
All except Gabe.
"Mrs. Lain," his voice soft and warm. "I'll get you up."
Up, I hobbled to the phone for a ride.
I realized later he didn't even ask for a late pass,
his free ticket into next hour late.
Remember the time the airplane crashed into the
*   Potomac in winter?*

People, warm, secure in travel itinerary one moment
the next dumped into teeth-chattering shock,
a nightmare of ice and bodies bobbing on gray water.
It was rush hour.
Cars banked up on the bridge.
People peered into swirling death.
One man, maybe others,
but one Gabe-like man whipped off his coat and
    jumped in
pulling people to warm blankets.
Gabe blushed when I told the class how he saved me.
Later,
when the room was empty,
he made me promise never to mention his kindness,
    please,
again in front of folks.

Gabe wouldn't hold still, stay in his box labeled "bigot." Teaching school means I'm constantly changing my definition of people. Gabe put himself out for someone, even if he had to suffer the consequences — tardiness and my public accolades. That's one kind of heroism, automatically risking your own skin to help someone.

Melissa Plugs Her Ears

Melissa just wouldn't heed anyone's advice.

I didn't even want to hear Melissa's talk — but talk she did. Her dad was Gone Johnson. Her mom tried to seduce Melissa's boyfriends. Melissa pulled me aside twice her senior year to tell me she was pregnant ... with different boyfriends. These were false alarms. Undaunted, she kept trying, and she succeeded. Six months later, when she walked across the stage to accept her diploma, she was showing.

> *Melissa*
> *You said you were going to have a baby*
> *twice before it really was true*
> *with first one post-high school boyfriend after another*
> *all adrift in a chemical sea.*
> *For the life of me I can't understand you*
> *setting the stage with your body*
> *for a lifetime of babies and men grabbing at your*
> > *breasts.*

The research paper stared Melissa in the face. She was supposed to study an author's life and work, and come up with a thesis. Preoccupied with her unborn child, she decided she wanted to focus her attention on how to teach her child values. Melissa and values seemed like an oxymoron. But just because her values eluded some, didn't mean she didn't have any.

Faced with her difficult situation, Melissa's character began to emerge. Together we wrestled with how to take her burning issue and apply it to the curricular requirement. She settled on this plan: she'd study a stack of children's books, including classics like *The Poky Little Puppy* and *The Little Engine That Could*. Then, she'd make a matrix with a list of values across the top and a list of children's stories down the left. She'd check off which stories dealt with which values. Still needing an author to study, Melissa came to me again. I mentioned Madeleine L'Engle, a writer with strong values. Melissa had read *A Wrinkle in Time* in junior high, and I recommended *Walking on Water*.

So she compared the values of kiddy lit with those espoused by L'Engle.

I liked Melissa's study almost as much as she did. The last time I saw her, she was taking classes at the community college, moving along toward a college degree, her little boy, Lars, in the college day-care program.

Melissa's choices might be unacceptable by community standards. After all, who could approve of her getting the cart of a baby before the horse of marriage and maturity? But then again, Melissa seemed to learn more when she jumped blind. She made messes and then learned as she cleaned them up. Thinking about Melissa, her leap-before-you-look attitude and the path she has now taken, I can almost feel my own tidy little beliefs crack like eggshells inside my skull.

Erik's Victory

For three weeks he looked at me with suspicious dark eyes and only pretended to write and read, even his self-selected stuff. I was not hopeful. I saw a tug-of-war coming, between Erik and me, between me and the counselor who would want to move him to the remedial class. But one day, Erik sort of mentally shrugged his shoulders and started writing. His favorite writing topic was his family, especially his grandma, the Queen of Homemade Tortillas, the Mother Teresa of scraped knees, the central figure of the family until her recent death. Erik and I began writing back and forth:

Erik,
struggler with conscience
("I will have my assignment in tomorrow.")
struggler with emotions

("*I feel depressed today.*")
struggler with values
("*I do not celebrate Christmas for religious reasons.*")
But the Erik I remember most
is a little black-haired boy
knees pumping
elbows chugging like pistons
uphill
to throw himself in Grandma's arms.
Later, when she died, he wrote about her
how he wished she were still around to catch him when
    he leaps.

Erik wrote back. A typical kid, he turned right around and handed me the blame that he hadn't gotten his act together in my class sooner. And he still harbored the notion that somehow, if he got enough extrinsic punishment, like spankings or F's, he'd be forced to behave and do the right thing. Then he could avoid the self-discipline and hard work inherent in being his own boss.

> *Mrs. Lain,*
>   *This doesn't have to be a thank you but it is anyway.*
> *I know I've been slacking off all year and I'm thanking*
> *you for putting up with my crap. You probably should've*
> *just flunked me for all of my late papers. From now on*
> *please do. Then maybe I'll quit messin' around.*
> *Erik*

Once in a while a boy like Erik will decide to get off his dead end and play along, participating instead of checking out. A change of heart is heroic.

MIGUEL LEAVES HIS MARK

Miguel was a hard worker with big dreams.

For three years Miguel and I met in the drive-through at Taco John's where he worked after school, me hanging out of my car window to talk to him. He wanted to get the Congressional Award before he graduated from high school, and he did. On Mother's Day of his senior year, he walked down the aisle in the rotunda of the Wyoming Capitol. U.S. Senator Malcolm Wallop placed the Silver Award over Miguel's head. He was honored for volunteering 300 hours at his elementary school and for setting other goals, like being the state president of the Higher Education Project and lifting enough weights to muscle up his marshmallow body.

Miguel was naturally good. He reminded me of a priest. I imagined him, brown robe roped at the waist, blessing people, his kind hands on bowed heads. He didn't plan to be a priest, though, but an engineer. Since nobody in his family had ever gone to college and few of his west-side neighbor kids had either, he would lead the way.

Miguel smiled a little when I gave him his poem.

You've made plans
from here to college.
Esperanza!
You figure out the writing assignment
and the steps through this school
to a mortar board crowning your dark head.
Esperanza!
I write your name on the line for Student of the Month,
Honor Society,
Congressional Award

and shine a flashlight beam ahead
as you pick your rocky way.
Esperanza!

What I didn't know was that Miguel had only a short time to live. He was murdered by a neighborhood kid, Sonny. After graduation, Sonny hauled groceries at Dan's County Market, while Miguel learned the ropes at the university. Was Sonny jealous, reasoning in his alcoholic haze that if Sonny couldn't go to college, neither could Miguel?

Miguel's friends from the campus Catholic center came en masse to the funeral. They played guitar and sang. One person after another eulogized him, saying how his life had been a blessing, a light, an inspiration. How he aced that last math test, how he made the Dean's List first semester, posted after his death. At his funeral, the parish priest said we must forgive Sonny.

The next summer I attended the same university. After I unpacked in my room at McIntyre Hall, I stepped out in lilac air. Spring comes late in the high plains. I glanced down at the wide expanse of sidewalk and suddenly remembered. This is the very spot described in the newspaper article. I pictured Miguel's brains airborne in the night sky, his blood spreading in a pool around his shattered head. I never crossed that sidewalk all summer long without remembering him, a lighthouse boy, a beacon of hope. A hero.

MARANTHA MAKES HER WAY

I thought about having Marantha move in with us. Gayle and I were walking around Sloan's Lake, watching the water ripple like horse flesh waving off flies. I mentioned her name to him.

Mara's large brown eyes observed our classroom, missing very little. She followed everything I said, supplying the words I lost between synapses. Following my train of thought, she was one of those students who could lead us back to the original question. Her quiet attention, like some invisible Elmer's Glue, held us together.

The outlet for her awareness was poetry. Gradually, she traded her large, round script for tighter cursive. Simultaneously, she graduated from her ninth-grade unicorns-and-roses themes to ideas like the elusiveness of beauty.

Mara was big on beauty, though she'd experienced plenty of ugliness. I think it was the guidance counselor who told the story. Mara and her two sisters were discovered in an apartment in Los Angeles. A social worker found them making an orderly life in spite of their mom's drug addiction. They rose and dressed themselves every morning and went off to elementary school, ready to please their teachers and avoid too much attention. Mara used the monthly child-support check to keep them in groceries. Their clothes were from Goodwill.

Then one day their mom awoke in the hospital after a blackout, maybe an attempted suicide. The existence of the three daughters came to the attention of the authorities, so the girls were sent to live with their dad in Wyoming. A recovering alcoholic, he nevertheless held a steady job as a postman. His live-in wasn't too thrilled about making room for three girls, but she agreed to give it a try. Hence, the girls became semipermanent house guests in their father's home, always polite as visitors should be.

I wondered what it would be like never to be at home enough to have a real knock-down drag-out with your siblings, the kind I had daily with one or two of my own sisters. What would it be like to confine your comments to pleasantries, even though adolescent rages and ecstasies roared through your veins struggling to vent? Did Mara ever sit on the floor of her bedroom and bawl, real loud, for no good reason? How did the girls get even with one another for wearing a hole in the only panty hose in the house? But this careful politeness to one another in a stranger's home kept a roof over their heads.

How Mara's eyes could be so calm and accepting I'll never know. She was a girl who bent to her writing with a kind of grace, her fingers smoothing the paper, her teeth gnawing her inner lip. Even though she secured her straight, brown hair behind her ears, it swung over the side of her face, affording her some private concentration.

I never took Mara home. It would have been OK with Gayle, but Mara and I were bound by our roles of teacher and student. Instead, I helped her publish her poetry in the Wyoming Arts Council literary magazine. I paved her way to attend the Upward Bound program at the nearby university—a summer school for at-risk students. I did these things, but she never got the mothering she deserved.

I looked her up at her high school. There was Mara, nine months pregnant and holding herself in firm control, even though my eyes filled with tears. A senior in high school, she moved out of her dad's house and set up housekeeping for her sisters and her baby. My journal jotting was as much a prayer as anything.

> *Marantha*
> *I saw you last week*
> *in the senior office*
> *my arms encircled you big belly and all.*
> *To the guidance counselor,*
> *you are a statistic called teen pregnancy.*

> *But in my ninth grade class you wrote poems,*
> *loved the whales,*
> *argued against abortion*
> *for you knew if your mother'd had the chance*
> *you'd not been born.*
> *You were almost predestined*
> *to bear the servitude of the load.*
> *But I know your baby*
> *will swim forth on a waterfall*
> *from your body*
> *you are his best hope to break the cycle*
> *of one man's blind urge to plant a seed anywhere*
> *and leave it unattended.*

We still write back and forth. She's working as a journalist in New Mexico and preparing her paperwork to reenter college, this time to become an English teacher. Invariably, her letters contain a picture of her son, Jacob.

WAKE UP AND LIVE

When I was in my early twenties, I almost died.

We were on our way back to the university for our senior year. In those pre-seat belt days, Darol, our first born, stretched out asleep between Gayle and me in the front seat of our Chevy Biscayne, an old guy's car, sort of thick around the middle. It was one thing we planned to replace when we graduated. We had big plans.

Our voices hummed along, soft as a baby's receiving blanket. Gayle talked about the stars, the theories of how the universe up there happened. We wondered how we fit into this giant scheme, Gayle and I sort of maverick twin comets. According to most people, we married too young, started our family before we could afford health insurance. We planned and wondered: Where will we student teach? How will we land a teaching job? Where will we live?

The badlands stretched out asleep all around us, no barn lights or house lights for miles and miles. The cars approaching us on the two-lane road were sparse, one every ten or fifteen minutes maybe, each appearing with two white lights like Little Orphan Annie eyes growing larger and larger, until in a puff of expelled breath, they whipped past.

Hell's Half Acre. That's a spot between the towns of Shoshoni and Casper. Miles of sagebrush, never touched by a white man's plow. Suddenly the earth breaks open into a giant earth crack, a small version of the Grand Canyon. Weird-shaped sandstone sentinels, carved by wind and biting blizzards, stand guard. No green thing lives in Hell's Half Acre, this eerie place where the earth threw a conniption fit.

That's where it happened. The highway rose up before us. We climbed the hill. Just at the lip, a car, its two lights already looming large, bore down on us on our side of the road. We had maybe two seconds to react; Gayle veered to go around and I laid down over my little boy's body.

My shattered pelvis hurt the worst. All the other broken bones took second place to that. The pain reminded me of the moment right before Darol pushed his little head out of the hoop of bone into the doctor's two waiting hands.

People appeared to help us. Gayle, sustaining head injuries of his own, assured me that our little boy was being warmed and comforted in someone's car. One man drove back 14 miles to Whitman, a town with a population of ten, to call for an ambulance. And I began to tilt my body so I could lie down in the car seat flat on my back, a position I'd occupy for almost three months of hospitalization.

The other vehicle was stolen, had no license plate. The drunk driver had no insurance and no driver's license. He walked away.

It was Thanksgiving when I came out of the hospital. The world was so bright I had to blink and shield my eyes with my hand. The air felt crisp, tart in my mouth like the first bite of an autumn apple. My salivary glands leak now, just remembering. "Earth, you are so beautiful it hurts," I thought. The feeling reminded me of Thornton Wilder's *Our Town*, a play read by every high school kid in the late '60s. In it Emily, who came back from the dead to revisit her life, said, "Oh Earth, you are too beautiful for anyone to realize you." She asked the stage manager if anyone really paid attention to their seconds and minutes and hours. "No," he said, "saints and poets, maybe. They do some."

The car wreck taught me how beautiful the Earth is. It helped define one kind of heroism — paying attention. Right in the middle of taking role: See how blue the sky is right outside the window? How sweet is an unpremeditated burst of laughter in the middle of silent reading? Instead of falling asleep at the desk, I learned to be utterly awake, to pay attention to students, as a teacher needs to do. Otherwise I could be a zombie, year after year listing kids' names in red gradebooks, filling in boxes in blue lesson planners, turning same pages in the purple *Elements of Literature* anthology, moving with the rhythm of the bell, marking my hours until retirement. That's one way to live. The car wreck taught me another. Wake up and live, as Emily said, "every, every minute."

I promised myself, though some part of me knew I couldn't keep it, that I'd never, ever forget to feel this freshness. It may have been at that moment that my own definition of heroism began to evolve.

We tend to think heroism means medals — the Silver Star, the Congressional Medal of Honor, the Purple Heart. But heroism can be feeling acutely alive in ordinary circumstances. It's as natural as flowers turning toward sunlight, like John and Miguel — both of them brightening the world by their presence. It's jumping in where angels fear to tread, like Gabe. Some people, like Marantha and The James, focus on a spot down the road and put one foot in front of the other. Some take the bull by the horns like Rex who saved his dad. Folks like Melissa respond to the urge to jump into apparent messes, and their heroism shines as they face the consequences. Heroism means coming to accept ourselves even when we don't fit in, like Dana. It means shaking off the mental muddle and choosing challenge instead of inertia, like Erik.

I write my students poems, not just to honor them or comfort them or nudge them or kick them in the rear. I give them poems so they'll be better readers and writers. They learn best by watching me demonstrate how to put into practice what I'm teaching them to know. I practice what I try to preach. Instead of mouthing the words love, respect, honor, comfort, I give away a poem. Besides feeding them a constant diet of grammar and authors and literary elements, so much wasted hot air after a while, I give away a poem. The concrete reality sinks inside like a stone, plunging to depths the lecture can't penetrate. Once they know this lesson in their bones, shushing the mental chatter about prom dates and tonight's big game and Friday's party and Jessica's new nail polish, they read with deep attention and real relish. They respect words, their own and other people's.

On the first day of school, I tell the students that once their names appear on my roster, we are stuck with each other.

They walk with me in the early morning as the sun lifts, they inhabit my dreams right alongside my own kids and husband. They pop in my mind's eye forever. They hear these words but don't listen. "Yeah, yeah," their bodies speak louder than words. But then I provide the solid proof for the claim: the poems. Those that splash cold water in the face. Those that cradle hope. Those that shelter the candle flame from the snuffing power of the wind. Those that weep and cheer, rant and rave. The poems are solid proof that the students — chirping, flitting, flying like chickens with their heads cut off — matter even in the crowded schoolhouse.

* * *

I pay attention to students, no matter how hard this is to do in our public secondary schools, to create a stronger sense of community. I build community to enable better teaching. If my curriculum were thin, having students memorize facts for multiple choice tests, asking safe little yes-no questions, then I probably wouldn't even need to learn my students' names, let alone create a safe haven in the classroom. But I teach students to read and write, to talk and listen, to connect big new ideas with their own experiences. To do this kind of deep learning, kids need to belong. To be named by the people around us is to be loved, and all of us learn to use language best through love.